Close
the
Wicket
Gate

JOHANNA O'MAHONY WALTERS

MERCIER PRESS
WHAT YOU NEED TO READ

Johanna O'Mahony was born in the Kilmichael Bar in Bandon
in 1946, the third of six children. She entered the Convent of Mercy
Kinsale in October 1965 - the year of her Leaving Cert. In 1974 she left
the convent and spent some time working in the Kilmichael Bar before
going to Wales and a teaching job in Milford Haven. She has lived there
for thirty years.

CONTENTS

FOREWORD

The Aborigines of Australia have the same word for past and present; it signifies 'the dreaming'. It makes sense.

Part of man's trauma is that very often he cannot fertilise the present. Too often he sees it when it has gone past. That is why even simple photographs take on a kind of magic as they age.

T.S. Eliot used to say that the function of art is to take the here and the now and make it rich and strange. I'm sure the author of this book would agree with the following lines:

> We look before and after
> And pine for what is not
> Our sincerest laughter with some pain is fraught
> Our sweetest songs are those that tell of saddest thought

The author grew up in Bandon a generation ago at a time when it was suffering from the general economic depression and from the loss of Allman's Distillery, a victim of Prohibition.

She got a great start in life: she got her early education in the family pub. A child wandering in a bar acquires a precious store of wide and varied knowledge.

A pub in those days was a kind of casual club. The publican was a man of many parts: he was captain of his ship; he needed to be knowledgable about many things, but especially sport; above all he needed to know those who could hold their drink and those who couldn't – and sometimes he had to slip a few pounds to a poor devil who had a cash flow problem.

His wife had to run functions: she heard confessions; she gave advice about many things, especially medicine; she was a counsellor before that profession was invented.

Philomena was further educated in the local convent. There she did her Leaving and thought about her future. The call to teacher training was the great prize of the time but she did not get it. It was hardly her fault: almost every night there were distractions in the pub; there were loud arguments about Hurling and Gaelic Football; somebody was playing at the piano; somebody was singing a little song of about forty five verses. The pub was hardly an institute of higher learning.

Philomena had now three choices – to get into the bank, train as a nurse or go to the university. None of those choices appealed to her. In her own words she decided to become a nun 'not because she wanted to but because she had to.'

She entered an order that stressed the value of meditation and the need to subjugate the self. Philomena tried diligently but for her the elimination of all hopes and dreams and desires proved impossible. She was a born rebel and a publican's daughter. She gathered up her courage and returned to the outside world.

This book tells the story of Philomena's early life with wonderful honesty; she goes on then and tries to capture the essence of her home town by concentrating on individuals – thus we meet the butcher and the teacher and the sailor and the soldier and the soldier's wife and the doctor and the musician and the miller and many more. We see Bandon in a clear but warm light – all of human life is there.

The great thing about this book is that Philomena sees into the kind of lives of which she had no first hand experience. That is the mark of a good writer. Her piece about the Irish emigrants in Britain is wonderful and as I can testify, very close to the bone.

I remember an evening long ago when I was in a pub near Buckingham Palace, sitting in the quietest corner I could find. It was about six o'clock and the bar was quiet except for three young West Indians who were playing with the gambling machine. A man came in and sat in the corner diagonally opposite me. He was middle sized and strongly built. He had brown red hair and the side whiskers that were then the mark of the Irish navvy. His brown boots were well decorated with the yellow clay of London. He took out his cigarettes and gave himself up to beer and tobacco. His face bore the imprint of many weathers. He could have been any age between 35 and

50. Once when he glanced up our eyes met fleetingly and I could hear him thinking 'I know you and you know me.' It was a moment of total communication. I worried about him. Would he go back to a cold flat or even colder lodgings?

I remember too meeting with emigrants who were too old to work. Often you would see them sitting in quiet corners in the pubs near Paddington Station and Euston Station, hoping to meet people from home or just to see them coming and going. They were sad men of quiet dignity; they would take a drink from you but always insisted in you having one back.

As I read this book I thought of a sentence from Thomas Hardy: 'At the grave-side of even the humblest man you see his life as dramatic.' Philomena, as she calls herself, has done us a great service.

~ *Con Houlihan*

INTRODUCTION

'The story of any town or village is the story of a nation in miniature' according to George Bennett who first wrote the history of Bandon in 1869.

Close the Wicket Gate takes a kindly look at life in Bandon during the 1940s, 1950s and early 1960s. Those far off days before mobile phones, emails, televisions and fast cars. Life was simple, people drew water from standpipes on the street, bathed in a tin bath beside open fires, cycled or walked to work, church and school and only business premises had telephones.

Families had large wirelesses in the corner and would listen to football and hurling matches on Sunday afternoons. 'The School around the Corner' with Paddy Crosbie was popular with the children who also danced to DinJoe's 'Take the Floor' on Wednesday nights. Sponsored programmes blared out at lunchtime – 'If you feel like singing, do sing an Irish song' was the advice of Walton's music programme. 'The Kennedy's of Castle Ross' kept us exercised as we waited for the fifteen minute daily episode. Lucky families had wind-up gramophones – all light years away from the experiences of today's young people.

Neighbours looked out for each other and provided help and support in the tough times. The extended family was a constant in the lives of young people.

These are gentle tales told with love and a good mixture of laughter and tears.

1

THE KILMICHAEL BAR

'Going, going … for the third time of asking … gone!'

Down came the auctioneer's gavel. So it really was gone. Sold to the man in the grey mac. He didn't look the type. A teacher, they said. What would he know about pulling pints? After thirty-four years it was gone out of the family with the goods and chattels which made up their 'home' sold to the highest bidder.

But times were changing. The old order was making way for the new. Business men and 'lounge bars' were killing the publican and the family pub. Pubs were becoming businesses, sidelines. No longer were they going to be a family's whole life as the KB – as it was affectionately called – had been to Phil's parents and siblings.

The locals who had watched the family grow up were, in a real sense, part of their extended family. They knew them as well as they knew their own children. The professor knew nothing of their history, their joys and sorrows, their quarrels and their loves; whole lives lingering in the smoky thermals of the Kilmichael Bar.

Philomena heard the news far away in Pembrokeshire. The telegram was brief: 'KB sold.' Her heart broke. This was her home. She had left it as a teenager but it was home. Where was home now? Here, in this hostile land, among these dour people – as she thought them at that time – people who never opened their hearts in welcome like they did back home? The pain was unbearable but who could she share it with? And who would understand? They knew nothing of her or her homeland.

Suddenly, for a moment, she was a child again, back in the bar in those comfortable, familiar surroundings, sitting on her low stool behind the wooden counter watching her mother, the landlady, filling pints and chatting easily with the punters. Her father, sitting in his usual corner by the window, joined in the 'ball hopping' as the general banter was called. Each one of the men (women did not frequent pubs in those days) was as familiar to her as her own uncles. Her brothers and sisters were busy filling shelves, doing homework, milking the cow or preparing the evening meal. And, once again, Phil heard the numerous tales – tall and otherwise – that lived and breathed in the bricks and mortar of the KB. The drinkers of the town could certainly choose bigger, more salubrious pubs, but none radiated the charm, love and camaraderie of the pub she knew as 'home'. She could still see the counter running from north to south along the length of the bar and the 'snug' found just inside the big window. The snug was a secluded little corner of the bar area where people who wanted a private drink could sit. Sometimes farmers' wives would sit in there and have a five-star port while waiting for their husbands who were enjoying themselves in the main bar. There were two kinds of port, three-star and five-star and a person's status could be determined by the variety they drank. Parallel to the counter ran the wooden bench which supported the barrels (also wooden). She relived the satisfaction of mastering the skill of 'tapping barrels' which she and her brothers and sisters had learned at a young age.

Outwardly, Phil did what so many Irish emigrants before her had done: she gritted her teeth and got on with her life.

2

THE LANDLADY'S TALE

'Two pints of Guinness, three pints of Murphy's, two halves of Carling, three halves of Paddy and two of Powers, please.'

If you can supply this order and calculate the cost without the aid of a calculator and without asking the customer to repeat it, you've cracked it. If you can also keep smiling and continue a conversation you really are in line for the 'Barperson of the Year Award'.

Stroll down memory lane to a small Irish town which, in the 1940s, could boast of sixty pubs. You had to be good to survive! The Kilmichael Bar, strategically placed at the eastern end of Bandon, was ideally positioned for the farming community to slake their thirst as they returned from creamery, fair, shopping or mass. Horses could be tethered to the telegraph pole outside the door or, if the horse was jittery, the reins could be held by the thirsty owner inside the pub! The street being wide, there was adequate parking for tractors, jeeps and cars.

In the 1940s, the profit on drink was so small that most pubs diversified and the KB was no exception: groceries were sold and a 'book' kept. Women came for their food during the week as they needed it and a list came in on Friday for the weekend order. The amount owed was entered in 'the book'. Phil can recall Fridays were extremely busy making up boxes of groceries and adding up the accounts which the men settled on their way home from work when they came for their 'couple of pints' before tea. Very often the boxes of groceries were delivered because so few people had their own transport.

The landlady kept a cow which enabled her to supply milk whenever anybody got 'caught out'. This was in the days before quotas, pasteurisation or milk lakes. The cow, a black Kerry, was beautiful. She grazed in the field behind the pub for part of the year and then, when the field was bare, she grazed on the 'long acre' which was about a half mile away, up Foxes Street. About five o'clock, the usual milking time, she would make her way back and bellow outside the gate until somebody let her in. It was part of the children's duties to milk this beauty. Sometimes, in winter, it needed two to perform the task – one to hold the light and the other to milk. Phil's brothers sang to her to enhance her milk producing capabilities!

In 1957, the opening of the cattle mart on the site of the old distillery (about a mile further east) greatly enhanced the already thriving trade of the KB. The landlady, being an enterprising woman, branched into catering, providing 'home from home' fare for the wider farming community as they came to buy and sell their livestock. Monday, the really busy mart day, brought farmers from a radius of about fifty miles. Phil has known Mondays when over 200 meals were served at this modest establishment. Of course, as children, she and her siblings had to peel potatoes and do the washing up – tasks they did not appreciate!

The building of a housing estate close by in the 1950s added yet another dimension to this already successful family pub. Of course these 'breaks' would not have been so effective had the landlady not been open to change and able to exploit each opportunity as it presented itself.

For the clientele, the pub was their second home. The landlady knew the favoured tipple of all her regulars and it was often even on the counter as they came through the door. This gave them a certain status over the 'passing trade' and over the farmers whose visits were more infrequent. In the pecking order, the locals were tops. Mostly they also had their own seats. Phil can see 'Johnny next door' sitting on his high stool at the corner of the bar with his half of Powers and pint bottle of Guinness in front of him, while Jack Shannon sat enthroned on the bench opposite the dart board, pint of Murphy's in hand, holding court.

The landlady was counsellor, friend, confessor and advisor to many of her customers and she treated their confidences with the greatest respect. She cared about what happened to them, helped financially or practically when she could and always provided a sympathetic ear. Many called her 'mother', such was her care for the drinking public. She made sure they did not spend all their wages for fear of letting their families go hungry. She told people when they had enough to drink and sent them home. Phil always marvelled at the respect these men had for this great lady. She feels it was because they mattered to her and they knew it.

Women did not frequent pubs in those days except on a very rare occasion. They would then indulge in a Winter's Tale sherry or a three- or five-star port! People's social standing was very much determined by what they drank. The majority of the men drank pints. Beamish and Murphy's, a brand of which was brewed locally, gave employment to many of these men; therefore, it was to their advantage to drink the 'home' brew.

The Irish pub was the 'training centre' where many a singer and musician served his apprenticeship. A sing-song could break out at the drop of a hat. The performer demanded an attentive audience. Nobody would dare talk during a song, re-citation, dance or musical piece. It did not matter whether the performer was good or not, he was encouraged to take part and as a result, his confidence increased. Once a performer finished, he had a 'worthy call' and a dim view was taken of anybody who didn't respond positively. Even the telling of a joke or story was acceptable but once called upon a person had to respond. The standard of entertainment was high in the KB. Phil can recall three occasions when it had the honour of winning the local singing pub competition. It was not only the singer who was considered, but the general atmosphere of the hostelry.

The licensing laws were bizarre in Ireland in the 1940s and 1950s. A person could not drink legally in his local pub on a Sunday – a closed day for pubs – but could travel to a pub three miles away and drink his fill. It had to do with the old idea of travelling on foot or horseback which was thirsty work. Because the opening times of the pubs were so limited they were completely ignored and no self-respecting drinker would be seen in a pub during the legal opening times. The result of this was a huge culture of after-hours drinking which would go on until the small hours of the morning. Saxy Dan, a stalwart of the KB, maintains that the children of publicans owe their education to after-hours drinking!

Owing to the scale of law-breaking by publicans, the gardaí were kept busy 'watching' pubs, while the publicans' children were kept busy 'watching' garda activity and warning of their imminent arrival. The gardaí would arrive on foot and could be seen from a long way off, giving the men time to vacate the premises, either via the wicket gate on to Foxes Street and safety, or through the other wicket gate and into the lane which led to the field. 'Don't forget to close the wicket gate!' the publican would yell as they left. The field – about two acres in area, situated behind the bar – could be accessed by a lane leading from the back gate of the shed. This nocturnal activity was a regular occurrence. The crime rate was very low in Bandon in those days and the boredom and monotony of being a garda on night duty was relieved by pub raids. The garda would enter the smoke filled bar, behold a blazing fire in the grate and not a person in sight! He would venture with his torch into the yard but, being unable to find anybody, would depart with a puzzled look on his face.

Then of course there was the phenomenon of 'invited guests'. The publican and landlady were entitled to have friends on the premises, but no drinks could be paid for. Any women who came with their husbands – usually the wives of returned emigrants – would be brought into the kitchen, where a tray of tea would be ready in case of an unexpected garda raid. It was a cosy sight that greeted the garda as he entered; up to ten women sitting around the kitchen fire sipping tea and chatting happily in the middle of the night – and this in the days before coffee mornings and lady's lunching became popular!

A rather bizarre episode relating to one of the KB's irregular customers did not have a happy ending. During the Christmas period he made a general nuisance of himself by drinking continuously for two weeks. He then went 'on the wagon' for the remainder of the year. On one particular night the KB was being raided by Garda McInerney who seemed to be acquainted with the geography of the place! The men were hiding in the back lane when this 'irregular' staggered up to the garda mistaking him for the landlord (who appeared when the coast was clear), put his arm around his shoulder and asked, 'Have they gone?' This resulted in a court appearance for the landlady, an endorsement on her licence and hefty fines for the 'found-ons'; those caught drinking after hours were known as the 'found-ons'.

With further changes in the licensing laws pubs shut at 10 p.m. on a Sunday. If the customers had food they could drink for a further hour. The enterprising landlady introduced soup and bread, which circumvented the law – inventing no doubt the phenomenon known as 'pub grub'. The landlady was summoned to court to answer the charge: 'Did soup and bread constitute a substantial meal?' She, of course, answered that it did. When asked by the judge what the ingredients were, she replied, 'That's a trade secret.' Back then the Irish had an innate distrust of the law. When confronted with what they considered a silly law they invariably found a way around it.

The late 1960s saw yet another change in the law which allowed pubs to remain open until 11 p.m. in winter and 11.30 p.m. in summer, with ten minutes drinking-up time. This ended the 'after-hours' drinking. Irish society was changing; pubs were becoming more 'professional' and businesslike thus losing the endearing quality of the family pub which had become such an institution. Still, Phil is glad to note that the landlady of the Kilmichael Bar retained her motherly attitude towards her 'boys' until her unexpected death in 1973.

3

The Publican's Tale

'It is not a suitable match, Neil,' reasoned his mother. 'I will not allow it.'

Nora, from the farm next door, was his cousin. His farm and Nora's farm had originally been rented as one by their great-grandparents who had been tenant farmers and when they died the farm was divided between their two children, a boy and a girl. The daughter, who married Neil's grandfather – a herdsman on the Swete estate – received the bigger share; a natural division being caused by a road. Both Nora and Neil's parents had been able to purchase their land in the 1890s under the Wyndham Land Act, which gave tenants the opportunity to buy their land over long periods of time.

Nora was ambitious; she liked the high life and enjoyed the good things in life, but she was also hard-working and had a good head for business. Neil's mother doubted she would settle down to being a farmer's wife and knew she wanted more for herself and for the children she hoped to have.

Neil had inherited his farm on the death of his father. A match had been planned between him and the daughter of a well-to-do farmer, a sensible girl with a good dowry, but he loved Nora and had done for years. Being neighbours they had known each other well since childhood. Their respective fathers, Paddy O'Mahony and Frank Buttimer, had also been great friends and had regularly taken off on horseback across the fields to the pub at Bengour or Coppeen to have a few drinks together.

So a match was made between Neil and Nora; everybody knew it was a love match and many wondered how it would work out for them. Nora had doubts about being the wife of a farmer and didn't feel she would be mistress of her own house with his mother and sisters still in residence. Neil knew this and spoke with his brother John, arranging for him to take on the farm, the mother and sisters. Soon after, he married Nora.

The newlyweds bought Miss Bannon's pub in Bandon, at Foxes Street Cross, allegedly named after George Fox, the founder of the Quakers who fed the hungry Irish during the famine. Well-intentioned country cousins wondered how Neil and Nora would manage to raise a family in such a place but Nora was feisty, capable and hardworking and determined to make both the marriage and the business work.

Neil bought a lorry and learned to drive; he was taught by Jerry Desmond, who worked in McGrath's garage in Boyle

Street and later moved to Thomas Carey's garage near the gasworks. Jerry also taught Nora and later four of their children to drive. Nora's driving career was short-lived however. One autumnal Sunday afternoon, while Neil looked after the bar, she took her family of four to visit their grandmother. The visit lasted longer than planned and it was almost dark when they left their Nan's house. Having learned to drive in the summer, she couldn't find the lights in the car, so she drove home at a snail's pace in the dark. The children were terrified. As it grew darker, Neil became concerned about his young family so he shut the bar and set off on foot towards the Dunmanway Road. When he reached Derrycool, he was relieved to see his lightless car coming towards him. In a state of panic Nora stopped the car and got out. She never drove again.

The publican, as he soon became known, used his lorry to transport livestock to horse fairs, cow fairs and all manner of livestock sales the length and breadth of three counties. His primary cargo was pigs, which he collected in dribs and drabs from various farmers. The pigs were taken to slaughter houses in Ballincollig, run by the Cork Farmers' Union, or to Denny's sausage factory in Tralee, or Evergreen, Murphy's bacon factory in Cork. The nature of this cargo, collecting a pig here and there, made the transport charges very difficult, if not impossible, to collect. Neil worked hard but was no accountant and in the end the business proved unviable and the lorry was sold. With the money from the sale he bought a car and worked painting cottages for the county council instead while Nora ran the business. This proved to be a much better arrangement.

Being a country boy Neil was never really partial to town life. Nonetheless, he always had a few pigs or chickens to look after and he was a keen gardener who continued to plant potatoes, onions, rhubarb and blackcurrant bushes in a corner of the field behind the pub.

In his younger days the publican was a fun loving man who liked to attend sporting activities: he belonged to the Bandon Athletic Club, liked racing and would regularly attend the Dunmanway Races on 15 August. He kept a beagle to go drag hunting during the season. On one occasion, while driving between Bandon and Ballineen en route to Ballineen races with Pat Wilmot and Jack Mahony, he hit and knocked down a donkey belonging to some travellers who were camping just outside the town. Garda Oates was called and the road was measured. The donkey was dead and there was slight damage to the car. The unfortunate travellers were charged with having animals unattended on the road and they had to dispose of their donkey.

The pub was fondly named the Kilmichael Bar, a link back to the publican and landlady's roots as both hailed from Kilmichael. The publican was not a political man, nor did he converse much about Irish politics, but he possessed a lot of knowledge about the Troubles having lived through them and been a member of the old IRA. It was known that he was involved in some skirmishes only by the fact that the black and tans stole his bike, a theft which really upset him as it was his main means of transport at the time. 'The Boys of Kilmichael' became the anthem of the KB and it was often heard wafting through the windows. Phil and her brothers and sisters were taken annually to Kilmichael on 28 November and to Béal na Bláth on 22 August just to show that their household supported both sides on the Civil War divide. The landlady and all her family were staunch Michael Collins supporters though and his picture hung proudly alongside one of the Sacred Heart and one of the pope on the kitchen wall of the KB – later John F. Kennedy was added to this distinguished gallery. Phil's dad, like many other people of the time, viewed the Civil War as an extremely sad period in Irish history and remained silent about it. Very often an argument would break out in the bar about the identity of Michael Collins' killer. This wound was still very raw in the Irish psyche in the 1950s so feelings ran high and the publican would have to intervene to restore order and to calm people down. He held the view that neither religion nor politics should be discussed in pubs as people held their views of both dearly and did not like to have them challenged.

4

THE NUN'S TALE

Before her final year at school, Philomena had never thought much about becoming a nun. She was part of the last generation of girls who had been taught only by nuns. From the age of five, when she first passed through the portals of the Presentation Convent school, until she left at the age of eighteen, all her teachers had been nuns. It had always been a cause of wonder to her as a small child that the nuns had no legs; they really did seem to glide along as if on wheels. Thanks to the rattling of their huge wooden rosary beads which hung from their leather belts their approach could always be heard long before they were seen. Cumbersome white head dresses and black veils hid their hair, foreheads and ears, leaving only their eyes, noses and mouths exposed.

It mystified Philomena that her brothers were taught by ladies in their infant school and gentlemen in their junior school. So teachers could be ladies, gentlemen or nuns? How could people who had other lives with wives, husbands, children, football coaching and the Gaelic League have time to teach? The nuns had only their prayers and their teaching and were not distracted by the stresses of raising families and training boys in the intricacies of football or hurling. Their whole lives were dedicated to their students' education and to their preparation for their future lives.

During her primary school years she liked the nuns and they liked her, especially the younger ones, the novices, known as 'postulants' and 'white veils'. They had a good sense of humour so she got away with a lot of talking and giggling. She could dance and act so she was always chosen to take part in festivals and concerts. Unfortunately, she could not sing in tune so she spent her school life mouthing the accompanying songs.

Irish was Phil's favourite subject; it was also the most important subject on the curriculum. After independence there was a desperate attempt by the new government, led by Éamon de Valera, to promote everything Irish and burn everything English except the coal. The Gaelic Athletic Association promoted Irish games and its members were, according to rule 27, forbidden from playing 'foreign games'. The Gaelic League promoted the use of the language; adult classes were held in the evenings; and the *fainne* (a silver or gold circle worn on the lapel), was awarded to those who achieved a certain standard in oral Irish. If you were unlucky enough to fail Irish in any of your examinations, you failed the entire exam, such was its importance.

On one occasion, when she was eight or nine years old, Phil was absent from school on the day the school inspector came to do an inspection; she did not enjoy good health as a child so was often absent. Sr Michael telephoned her mother to ask if Phil could come to school just for that day as, being a confident young madam, she could be relied on to answer questions. Her father drove her which was unheard of because nobody was ever driven to school back then even though the Kilmichael Bar was a good mile from her school and it was mostly up hill. She was seated in the front row where she got picked on frequently by the inspector as she waved her arm in the air ready to answer his many questions on poetry, stories and grammar. Sr Michael was delighted with her performance and telephoned her father to come and take her home.

Priests regularly visited school and talked of the evils of drink or the 'demon drink', speaking of pubs as if they were dens of iniquity. This disturbed Phil as she loved her home and had been, up until that time, unaware that it differed from those of the other girls. It was common practice to take the pledge as part of the confirmation ceremony; this was a promise not to drink alcohol until the age of twenty-one when you were enrolled in the Pioneer Total Abstinence Association and could make a commitment to abstain from alcohol for the rest of your life. It was difficult for Phil to understand how you could give up something you had never even tasted.

Phil lost many of the girls who had been her companions in primary school when she moved to secondary school. Education was not free in Ireland in those days which meant a small fee had to be paid if you wanted to go to secondary school. Sadly, even this small contribution prevented many young people from having second-level education. Many of her friends had to remain in primary school until they reached the school leaving age of fourteen before going to work or, in many cases, 'taking the boat', as emigration to England was called.

Girls from the surrounding country schools joined Philomena in secondary school. They cycled or came by the regular town bus service, as it was the age before school buses; free education, along with school buses, only came to Ireland in 1967. These girls were known as 'the country girls' and were much favoured by the nuns, many of whom were 'country girls' themselves. Some of the girls had to leave home before eight o'clock in the morning to get to school on time. Regardless of the weather, summer and winter, they undertook this journey, often in the dark because school did not finish until four o'clock. They sometimes arrived in school soaked through and had to sit in wet clothes all day.

The logo on the school uniform was PCB, Presentation Convent Bandon and it had to be worn with honour and respect (students from the other schools in town called its wearers 'public cheeky brats'). Walking in the main street too often, talking to boys or carrying plastic bags (which had just been introduced by the grocery shops) while wearing the PCB uniform was considered a real crime. This often resulted in a good smack on the hand with the leg of a chair, which in some ways was better than 'the verbals' which seemed to go on forever, or the flying board duster which you had to duck to avoid. Often the girls from the town were referred to as 'townies' or 'street walkers'.

It always amazed Phil that the nuns – who never left their convent – were so well informed about the 'high jinks' of their students. Of course, they had their 'informers': ladies who were regular visitors to the convent and relayed all the gossip to any sister who was prepared to listen; a few refused to engage in any gossip about their charges. The girls from the country were lucky in that they lived far enough away for their misdemeanours not to be discovered.

Phil didn't perform as well in secondary school and unfortunately, the nuns who now taught her were not as indulgent as those she had encountered in the primary school. She did the minimum amount of study needed to pass her exams and was often scolded for her lack of effort. There were so many interesting things happening at home in the KB that Phil was regularly distracted from her homework. Jimmy might be singing one of his ancient ballads which consisted of about forty-four verses, an argument might have broken out among the card players, or Mickey might be playing 'Some Enchanted Evening' on the piano. Any of these diversions would easily lure her from 'the books'.

In secondary school a different nun taught each subject which was a big change for Phil who had been taught by the same nun during her final three years in primary school. Sr

Alphonsus was an inspired teacher and good fun, sharing many a joke with her class. Generations of Bandonians benefited from her amazing talent and hard work. But now Phil had to get used to more serious-minded nuns. Of course, preparing young girls for the public examinations was quite a serious matter. The intermediate certificate, taken in the fourth year and the leaving certificate, in the sixth year, comprised nine or ten subjects respectively. All subjects were compulsory. There was no such thing as a free period.

All this hard work, including attendance at school on a Saturday morning, left little time to contemplate the future. The high-flyers would go to teacher training; that was the goal of the nuns, as schools were judged by the number of students who were 'called to training'. The matriculation could be bought if a student had sufficiently good grades in the leaving certificate so that put university in second place. Then there was nursing or the bank. Those were the choices. Failing the leaving certificate was not an option: it would bring disgrace on yourself, your family and the school. According to the nuns, if you worked hard and did as you were told, you would pass and that was that. There was huge pressure on the students, even though the education of girls was not considered very important as they would marry anyway and be kept by their husbands. Jobs such as teaching, nursing and the bank did not employ married women.

Phil had no idea what to do with her future. Since she could neither sing nor sew teaching was out of the question and anyway, she did not feel drawn to it. Like the other girls in the class of 1965, she had listened to and watched many presentations about the missions when the various religious congregations had come to the school on their recruiting campaigns. There were many such congregations: Our Lady of the Apostles, the Medical Missionaries, the Franciscans and the Sisters of Mercy. These orders had sisters working in Africa, South America and Asia as well as in America, Australia and England.

Phil's cousin had gone with the Presentation Sisters to work in Texas but Phil did not consider that as real missionary territory. She was more drawn to the southern hemisphere and the 'Black Babies' who had been so much a part of her life ever since she had started school and she and the other girls had brought in their pennies for these babies who had captured their imaginations. Some nuns had spent their whole lives working among the poor in their villages and shanty towns. They had founded schools, hospitals and clinics in the most unlikely places for the benefit of the underprivileged. Phil was filled with admiration for the dedication and self sacrifice of these women and wondered what it would be like to be part of that wonderful adventure.

She, like many of the young girls of her time, was idealistic and believed she could save the world. She imagined herself working among the poor and deprived in some faraway exotic-sounding place. It held a certain glamour for her. She never gave much thought to the kind of work she might do, except that she could never be a nurse, having no stomach for all that blood and vomit. She was so wrapped up in her thoughts of being a missionary and a nun that she drifted into the convent without too much soul-searching or giving much thought to the day-to-day living of a religious life. She knew she did not want to join the nuns she had been educated by as they were a teaching order and their mission was in Texas. She was introduced to the Sisters of Mercy by the school chaplain who had an aunt and a sister in the order.

The Mercy congregation was founded by Catherine McAuley in Dublin in 1831. Catherine was an extraordinary woman, a rich heiress who devoted her whole life and fortune to the care of the poor, sick and uneducated. The Mercy congregation spread rapidly under her inspired leadership. She was a woman well ahead of her time and her nuns were called 'walking nuns'.

In the 1880s, nuns were not seen in public so the Sisters of Mercy caused quite a stir by being found in the homes of the sick, the hovels of the poor and wherever they were needed. They set up schools, hospitals and orphanages as well as laundries and sewing rooms for the employment of young girls. The lace-making industry in their convents became quite famous, especially Kinsale Lace, originally introduced from Limerick. It was fashionable for rich ladies to choose garments made from this lace as part of their marriage *trousseau* (trunk). In 1899, a request for a baby's shawl came from Windsor Castle to the Kinsale Convent with the payment of five pounds and ten shillings. Sadly, the lace workroom ceased operating in the 1950s and with it this beautiful skill was lost.

Phil's friend, Mary O'Donoghue, who had been a year ahead of her at school, had just joined the Mercy congregation. Phil visited the convent a few times, met some of the novices and the novice mistress and was accepted for a probationary period. Joining the Mercy congregation was something she felt, deep in her soul, that she had to do rather than wanted to do. It seemed so right.

Her family, particularly her mother, did not take the same view. The landlady felt that Phil would be more useful in the world instead of shutting herself away in some convent never to be heard of again. Why not go to university and get a degree, see a bit of life and if she still felt the call, she could enter then? Her mother was a wise woman as convents nowadays no longer accept girls straight from school; they need to have some experience of life before they enter. But Phil was determined and her family relented. Having a priest or nun in the family was quite a status symbol in Ireland. The belief was that if you had a bull in the field, a pump in the yard and a son or daughter in the diocese you had reached the social Mecca. Her family was unique in that they did not worry about this social perk.

A list of requirements arrived from the convent: three of everything, one to wear, one at the wash and one set aside for an emergency. She went to Cork with her mother to shop for her *trousseau* and when all the bits were assembled they were locked in a big trunk and delivered to the convent to await Phil's own arrival.

As 31 October drew closer Phil began to feel a nagging pain in the pit of her stomach. She wondered whether she had made the right decision. Well, it was too late now to turn back so she dismissed these fears and got caught up in the excitement of the adventure: people were coming to say goodbye, wishing her well and praising her choice of career.

She found herself togged out in a postulant's outfit – a long black dress, stiff white collar and cuffs and the bonnet – before she woke up to the fact that this was for real. The 'bonnet' – a trial to anybody's vocation – was a frilly halo surrounding the face with a bow tied under the chin and a piece of black net at the back.

Her family sat in the huge convent parlour with its beautiful old solid furniture, sniffling, fighting back the tears. A picture of Pope Paul XI and another of the local bishop, Cornelius Lucey, smiled benignly at them from the back wall. She found it difficult to look at her sister, Marion, who was eleven, or her little brother, Barry, who was only eight. She knew she would miss out on their lives and that hurt. Her other sister and two brothers had a shared history and childhood with her and she would miss them also, but she had the compensation of happy memories of their time together. The little ones were so much younger. She would have liked to have had more time to become part of their lives. She had never seen her big, strong dad, her brothers and sister look so sad and uncomfortable. Even her brother's efforts at derogatory comments about her postulant's bonnet sounded hollow. Her mother seemed to be the only person coping with the situation even though her eyes also glistened. It was like a wake. The big heavy wooden doors banged behind them and then they were gone.

Kathleen and Sheila entered the convent on the same day. Kathleen was twenty-seven and had longed to be a nun for many years but had been prevented from doing so by poor health. She seemed old to Sheila and Phil; normally, girls entered convents straight from school but Kathleen was older than all the other novices. Sheila, aged eighteen, had come straight from the convent boarding school. All the novices, except Mary, were past pupils of the boarding school attached to the convent; Mary had entered six months earlier and was still a postulant. She was a 'Pres' girl like Phil. The other novices, eighteen in all, were a kind and jolly bunch and Phil and her two companions were enveloped into this happy family.

The first meal in the convent was extraordinary. Being Hallowe'en, the Celtic festival of Samhain, there were apples, nuts, ginger biscuits and the traditional barmbrack. Phil sat at the end of the novices' table in a state of bewilderment. She had never seen so much black and white, or heard so much banging and clanging of crockery; there must have been over fifty sisters in the refectory. Not having been to boarding school Phil found this experience of communal eating strange.

The refectory was set out rather like it would be for a wedding with a top table accommodating the reverend mother, her assistant, the bursar and the novice mistress and the other tables coming down on either side with the sisters seated in order of seniority. There was a great empty space in the middle of the floor for the servers to move about freely. The novices sat at the end of a long table under the keen eye of the novice mistress. The poor woman turned various shades of puce as her charges laughed too loudly, overfilled their mouths, had their elbows on the table or looked about too much. She took each of these transgressions in decorum personally. The reverend mother, a jolly woman with a warm and gracious nature, rang the bell to announce that she had found the ring in the barmbrack.

After supper the novices and postulants were granted the special concession of watching television for an hour. The bell for night prayer rang at nine o'clock, marking the beginning of the great silence which would continue until after breakfast the following morning. The new recruits were exempt from spiritual exercises during their first week while they became familiar with their surroundings, so that first night they were shepherded to the organ gallery to say a brief prayer and then on to bed.

The most frightening thing for Phil on that first night was going down to her cell to bed. It was small, spartan and eerie with huge wooden shutters. It housed only a bed, a chair, a cupboard and a jug and basin on a stand. Bare boards, a crucifix and a small picture of Catherine McAuley completed the furnishings.

The novices had their own wing which included the noviceship – a room where they studied, listened to lectures and spent their time when they were not in choir or doing their household chores. Each novice had her own place around a huge table. Novices sat in order of seniority each having a writing desk and a drawer containing her few belongings.

The main part of the convent building was very impressive with high ceilings and wide corridors. Niches containing statues adorned the corridors. The gardens were expansive and elegant with plenty of walking space for the nuns to say the 'walking rosary', a prayer with which Phil was unable to come to grips. She was attracted to meditation but could not manage to marry the meditation on the mysteries to oral prayer. The rosary consists of fifteen mysteries meditated on in rotation: five joyful, five sorrowful and five glorious. Each mystery depicts an event in the life of Jesus. While meditating on these, the decades are recited. Each decade consists of ten 'Hail Marys' with the 'Our Father' at the beginning and the 'Glory be to the Father' at the end.

The rosary has been said in many Irish families for generations but in the KB it was hit or miss whether the family rosary was recited or not. Perhaps her difficulty with the rosary had something to do with her youth in Gurranreigh where she spent her holidays on her grandmother's farm and disrupted the rosary with her giggling and giddiness, accordingly spending more time in punishment outside the back door than on her knees in the kitchen.

Phil's first week as a postulant went by in a haze of loneliness and grief. She could not bear to look at the children in the senior infants' class where she encountered a seven-year-old boy who looked so like her little brother Barry that every time she saw him she dissolved into tears. She slept little, weeping for her family and her home as the grim reality of what she had done set in. She wanted to go home and begged her mother to come and get her, promising to work full time in the KB 'for free' but her mother reminded her of her heroic uncle who had emigrated to America fifty years previously and was so homesick that he had not dared to come home since.

Two weeks into her religious life disaster struck. Kathleen died. She felt ill at supper on the Sunday and was sent to bed. By nine o'clock, when her companions were going to bed, she was in severe pain. The doctor was called and she was moved to the infirmary. The following morning while awaiting the ambulance to take her to hospital she passed away. The one consolation for those who knew her was that at least she had got her wish: she lived the life of a Sister of Mercy, if only for two weeks. A small white cross in the cemetery bears witness to the short-lived religious life of this gentle and loving soul who so desperately wanted to devote her life to God.

The shock and panic left the novices reeling with fear. The novice mistress had to babysit them until quite late every night for weeks afterwards. Often they sneaked into each other's beds and slept together for comfort. The need for warmth and human companionship was intense.

Gradually, things began to stabilise and routines were established. The rising bell rang at 6 a.m. and after a quick wash in cold water, the novices dressed and were in choir by 6.30 a.m. to start the day's prayers. Mass was at 8 a.m. after office (liturgical prayer of the church) and meditation. Breakfast followed mass and then it was on to the day's activities. Every day followed a regular pattern which varied only during holidays or in the wake of some extraordinary happening. Phil began to long for such happenings to break the monotony of day after day of such boring regularity. She longed for adventure, surprises, anything that would alter the pattern and vary the routine.

At one level, she wanted to be a good nun, but at another she did not want to lose her identity and of course, she was used to so much variety in the KB where she never knew what might happen from one minute to the next. In the convent conformity was required: 'Walk without swinging your arms', 'Keep custody of the eyes' and regular reminders of the need for 'decorum' – whatever that was!

She was accepted into the order. She had hoped she would be but wondered if her lack of practical skills would come against her. Her reception ceremony was simple, private and beautiful. The bishop celebrated the mass. Halfway through the service her hair was cut as a symbol of her withdrawal from the world. She was dressed in her cap, dimity (worn under the veil) and white veil. She was also given a new name. She had been given her grandmother's name at her baptism and would have liked to have kept it, but the custom then was to be given a saint's name. Many nuns have gone through life bearing a male name so at least she was lucky to be given the name Gertrude. Her family came to visit in the afternoon. It would be their last visit for six months as she now entered the spiritual year when she lived a fully contemplative life.

Her day was now taken up with study of the rule of the congregation, prayer and meditation. She really was on her way to becoming a fully fledged nun; moreover, she rose to the challenge. She loved the peace and tranquillity of this year and she learned much about the work of the order. Following her spiritual year she got involved in the secondary school, teaching English, civics, religious education and speech and drama. She enjoyed working with teenagers since they appealed to her more creative self.

Phil's house duties included some cleaning of corridors from which she graduated to the choir, which was separated from the chapel by a huge iron grille. The sisters did not use the chapel; it was for the lay people including the girls from the boarding school, who attended mass at the convent. Each sister had her own choir stall which she used for all her spiritual exercises including the recitation of the office, in Latin, five times a day. This was where she was engaged, doing the Saturday cleaning, when her grandmother died at the age of ninety-seven. She was allowed to leave the convent in the company of her new novice mistress, Mother Finbarr, to attend her Nan's funeral. However, being still a novice, she could not visit the KB which she passed on the way. Of course it was closed because of the funeral but it still felt strange driving past without stopping.

She did a stint of duty in the community room with the indomitable Sr Raphael who was such a character. Sr Raphael had never got bogged down with the minutiae of religious life. She continued to brim over with fun and good humour. She wore rouge and appeared in high-heeled shoes, even when she was quite an old lady. She was an amusing sight tottering to 'the parlour' to greet a visitor or adventuring on a day at the seaside. She also entertained the community with her antics on feast-days. She was loved by young and old.

The main purpose of all the activities, prayer, study, work and reading, was to bring the will into submission or, as we call it today, the death of the ego. A sister needed to be compassionate, able to reach out in love to others and to put her own needs last. Self-love or self-advancement was the enemy of holiness. Obedience was all important; 'blind obedience', as it was called.

After two years as a white veil, Phil made her first profession. She took temporary vows for three years – poverty, celibacy, obedience and the service of the poor, sick and ignorant. Most religious congregations take three vows, but the Mercy congregation have always taken this fourth vow of service. As a temporary professed sister, she was given a black veil. This was the time when novices were sent to train as teachers or nurses and Phil was sent to Newcastle upon Tyne, to a college of education run by the Sacred Heart sisters. The requirement of candidates for teaching was less stringent in England than in Ireland. Phil could dance and act and furthermore, the grades she had achieved in English, Latin and maths qualified her for a place on the teacher training course.

She felt rather like a parcel. She had scarcely been outside the convent walls since she had entered four years previously and now she was on an aeroplane bound for a foreign land. She had chosen drama and dance as her main subjects, hardly an obvious choice for a nun. Special permission was secured for her to wear clothes compatible to these activities. Luckily, drama was a subject pursued by few – there were only fifteen students in her year group – and they were all kind and considerate towards her. Of course, having a nun on the course must have been something of a novelty.

For the duration of her college career she managed the drama department's seven-a-side football team. The fact that she knew nothing about soccer did not seem to matter. They were a good team and won the interdepartmental competition two years running and the intercollege competition another year. When she returned to her convent the team's captain gave her a gold medal he had won as a leaving gift.

She enjoyed her college course and even grew to like the teaching. She worked hard and graduated three years later as a fully fledged teacher. She had grown up in the three years, having been exposed to many experiences and having to take responsibility for her actions in the absence of her superiors. She made her final profession and committed herself to the Mercy congregation with confidence when she returned to her convent. She was eager to get on with her religious life and her teaching, but soon discovered that returning to the convent was like stepping back in time. She had been living life as prescribed by the Second Vatican Council while in Newcastle and so found it impossible to cope with the lack of progress in her own community.

Back in 1974, the whole Catholic Church was in turmoil and the religious communities reflected that. There was a tug-of-war between the old and the young, the former trying to 'do what was always done' while the young were looking for challenge and a channel for their boundless energy. People on all sides acted from purely honourable motives; they believed they were doing God's will as they saw it. Many nuns left at that time, some of whom were excellent teachers and deeply spiritual people, committed and dedicated to the education of the young.

The mirage of the missions had slipped further and further away from Phil. It now looked hopeless. She would never be chosen to serve in South America where the diocese had a parish. The bishop told her he wanted 'good' nuns which seemed to rule her out. She was too much of a rebel and too outspoken. After almost a year, seeing no light at the end of a dark tunnel, she applied to Rome asking to be dispensed from her vows. It was with great sadness that she left her home of the past ten years and faced the great unknown.

It has been said by some sisters that Phil closed the convent door behind her when she entered because no novices arrived after her. The old convent building is now no more. It has been sold to a developer and the remaining twenty nuns have moved into a lovely purpose built comfortable home overlooking Kinsale town and harbour.

5

The Emigrant's Tale

It has been said that Ireland's greatest export has been her people. In every part of the planet the Irish or their descendants can be found. Emigration has been romanticised in song and story and so much written about that they are now referred to as the diaspora. During the 1940s and 1950s emigrants were prayed for at the end of every mass. People were leaving by the boat-load, much to the government's relief; it was an easy solution to the unemployment difficulties. Families were split when the father had to emigrate to find work to feed and clothe his wife and children at home. Some fathers were never heard of again; they met and married women in England and forgot about those they had left behind, neither family knowing about the other. Untold hardship was suffered by the families left abandoned in Ireland.

De Valera's romantic notion of little homesteads on the hillsides with lights in the windows was just that – a romantic notion. People were uprooted from their native soil, from places of extraordinary beauty like Kerry, West Cork, Connemara, Donegal and all the other wild and wonderful parts of Ireland. These places, now made rich and famous by the Tourist Board are where the vast majority of people emigrated from as they could not eke out a living from the poor land. Ireland's emigrants were transported from these spirit-enhancing beauty spots into the centre of some of England's most industrial cities: rolling hills replaced by grey skyscrapers, shimmering lakes replaced by smelly rivers and canals. Many lodging houses in these cities carried notices proclaiming 'No blacks, no dogs and no Irish'. No wonder many of our emigrants found refuge in the pub among their fellow countrymen where they could talk and sing of home.

Sociological and psychological studies have shown the effects on people of displacement. The pattern is the same in the stories of the Aboriginal peoples of Australia and New Zealand, of the American Indians and of course, in the tales of our own refugees from the famine, as well as in those of our present-day political and economic refugees. People lose their identity and their sense of belonging. The intense pain of not belonging in the host country and no longer belonging in the homeland has to be felt to be understood; every emigrant will relate to it. Songs such as 'The Mountains of Mourne', 'Remember Laddie, he is still your Daddy', 'McAlpines Fusiliers' and 'If we only had old Ireland over here' are but a few of the thousands of ballads sung by those who longed to be at home.

Phil's godfather, her uncle Maurice, experienced all of this. He left his small farm in West Cork in the 1950s for a job with Tarmacadam in Birmingham. He stayed with Billy – a neighbour's son – and his wife for a week until he 'settled in' and got a place to stay: a room in the home of Jack and Jane from Mayo. He tried about twenty places before he found them but had the door slammed in his face. His home in Ireland had welcomed everybody and entertained visitors from all quarters of the globe so he could not understand this lack of welcome. His room, in a house on a road just off Spark Hill, was small and gloomy. In his little space of twelve foot by nine foot he cooked, ate, slept and read the *Southern Star*, which his sister sent him faithfully every week. He was a scrupulously clean man and managed to keep this 'box' neat and tidy. He had the use of a bathroom which he shared with the family and the two other men who had 'rooms' in the house.

Some of the landladies at the time were tough women. Many were Irish women who had come over a few years earlier and had made some money, but who now had no scruples about exploiting the young greenhorns from Ireland, charging high rents for very little facilities. Some of the lodging houses were filthy and often up to four or five men would occupy a single room. One man tells the story of five young men from West Cork who went together to London to work for McAlpine and were housed in one of these establishments. On the first morning one called to the others that it was half eight, time to get up, to which one of the young wits responded: 'I'm all ate – with fleas!'

Maurice ate well. He bought a joint of ham on a Saturday, cooked it in a big pot with potatoes, carrots, parsnips and cabbage and ate it during the week as well as having sandwiches for work: great thick 'doorsteps' with the ham in between. He sent home a chunk of his wages to support the family while he lived a miserable life going from work to the room to the pub, with the diversion of mass on Sundays. He was always faithful to Sunday mass, as were most of the emigrants. Very often they were lucky to find a sympathetic young Irish priest who understood them and their difficulties.

He was a fun loving man, who did not seem to have any responsibilities and he had the quaintest of expressions, such as 'We'll take lots of no notice'. 'How do' would preface anything he didn't like or considered not up to standard: 'How do "main door", there is only one door in this hotel,' he boomed, on being asked where the main door to a particularly dilapidated pub was. Noticing a lady relative in a large John Wayne type hat at a funeral his caustic observation was, 'She should have first got a head'. He never cared whether his remarks were overheard or not. As a confirmed bachelor, he despised men who were, as he thought, ruled by 'petticoat government'. He could never have been a supporter of the feminist movement.

The highlight of his year was the return home for the summer and Christmas holidays. He arrived like Santa Claus with presents for everybody. His mother lived for his return, as did his sister and brother and later his nieces and nephews. It was the publican's job to collect him from the airport and transport him home to his mother's farm – a lengthy business. On his arrival at the Kilmichael Bar he bought drinks for all who happened to be already ensconced there. This seemed to be the pattern with all the emigrants: their pride was such that they wanted to give those 'at home' the impression that they were doing very well, that the streets of England's cities were indeed paved with gold. They had a constant entourage of 'hangers on' while they were home and spent all their hard-earned money buying drinks for these 'friends'. Before their return, inevitably, they would run out of money and have to borrow from the landlady so as not to lose face. Then they would return to England, work hard to repay their loans and save for the next 'holiday'.

Having satisfied his thirst in the KB, Maurice's journey to Gurranreigh would begin. As a pub could not be passed without a stop, it was a good thing that there were only two. Again Maurice would buy drinks for the assembled drinkers; it didn't matter whether he knew them or not. By the time he reached home, both he and the publican were well inebriated – not that it lessened the warmth of Maurice's welcome. While at home, Maurice rode an old rusty bicycle and visited the neighbours and relatives aboard this rusty mode of transport. The pub was visited every evening and he took many a tumble on the inebriated return journey. Once he was stopped by the gardaí because he didn't have a light: 'Where is your light, Sir?'

'Up there,' he answered, pointing to the moon, 'where's yours?'

After some more incoherent mutterings from Maurice, the gardaí decided to abandon the task of arresting him for being drunk in charge of a bicycle and for having no light. By some miracle he arrived home without further incident.

Life was such in rural Ireland in the 1950s that all the returned emigrants would visit each of the neighbours in turn. Every household had family in England, America and Australia. Those in England came regularly, but those further afield came every four or five years. These 'yanks' caused great excitement and questions such as 'Have the yanks called on you yet?' would be asked of each other at mass or at the creamery. Cakes would be baked ready, in case they came, as indeed they always did. Twelve of Maurice's father's family had emigrated to America so there was a constant flow of yanks to the farm; these were either their own relatives, or their relatives' friends whom they would have asked to visit the folks at home.

Some of those who left Ireland in those days lost touch with their families. Maurice was instrumental in reuniting one such family. Jim Coakley, who was in his seventies, had left a farm near Dunmanway when he was nineteen, worked all his life in England and had never returned. The family at home spent many years trying to trace him but failed, a cause of great sadness on both sides. Maurice's grandmother was a Coakley. One day while reading the *Southern Star* – his main link with home – Maurice read of the death of a Mrs Coakley from near Dunmanway. After mass in Spark Hill the following Sunday, he mentioned this to Jim who replied, 'That's my mother'. There and then Maurice decided that he would bring this poor man home on a visit; Jim's sister, Mrs Donovan – Saxy Dan's mother – lived just a stone's throw from the KB. There was terrific excitement and partying at Jim's return, tinged of course with sadness that his mother was no longer alive. Jim returned each year from then until he died and Maurice continued to visit his sister and bring her snuff until she died.

Gambling was a great hobby of Maurice's and he loved to go to the races. Having sustained heavy losses at Cheltenham in 1979 he suffered a severe stroke which rendered him speechless. He lay all night on the floor until his landlady discovered him in the morning. He was taken to hospital where he was badly cared for. Phil and her husband found him unshaven, drooling and unable to speak, in filthy pyjamas, smelling of urine and crying. They were utterly devastated by the distress in which they found him and they immediately went off to get pyjamas, toiletries and other necessities for him. By the time they returned from shopping he had been tidied up and looked better.

Eventually he recovered sufficiently to leave hospital and go to live with Phil and William in Wales. He went into sheltered accommodation close by after about a year and was well cared for by the matron and staff. He never regained his speech but he enjoyed a reasonable quality of life, backing horses, having pints and walking to mass, until his death in 1988.

A requiem mass was celebrated for him in the parish church he had attended during his eight-year sojourn in Wales. There was a large attendance as he had become well known and well liked in his adopted home. His remains were put on the afternoon ferry from Fishguard and accompanied by Phil and William, he set sail on his final journey across the Irish Sea. On the journey from Rosslare the hearse 'flew' on the open road causing the solitary mourning car great difficulty in keeping up. However it slowed down and drove respectfully going through towns and villages, while the people stood and blessed themselves, men removed their hats and caps and traffic stopped to allow a clear passage for this unknown corpse. The cortège stopped at his nephew's house in Glounthaune so he could join the procession and the drivers and mourners could have a cup of tea. This caused consternation among his nephew's neighbours when they saw a hearse parked in his drive at ten o'clock on a September evening.

When the cortège arrived at the church at eleven o'clock that night, people poured out of the three pubs in the village and within minutes the church was packed to overflowing. He certainly got a good reception. After the rosary, it was back to the pub for the wake, which didn't end until after 3 a.m. The following afternoon at the burial it was the same routine: the pub, the church, the cemetery and back to the pub. Crowds of people – family, relatives, friends of his youth, people who had not seen him for many years – came in their droves to pay their respects, or was it to attend the social event? It is well known that a good funeral is better than a bad wedding. This man who had such a lonely life since his stroke now seemed to have thousands of friends. Why could some of them not have visited him during the previous eight years? And what had become of his Birmingham friends? He had lived there for nearly thirty years.

6

THE TEACHER'S TALE

In the 1940s and 1950s, education in Ireland was a privilege available only to the few who could afford it. It was provided mainly by the religious congregations who were founded for that purpose. The boys of Cork city and some towns throughout the county were served by the Presentation, Christian and De La Salle Brothers, with special mention of the Junior Seminary at Farranferris – the cradle of priests and hurlers! The Sisters of Mercy, Presentation and Ursuline Sisters provided education for the girls.

In Bandon, while the girls were educated by the Presentation Sisters who arrived there in 1829, there was no provision for secondary education for Catholic boys before 1940. The families who could afford to educate their sons sent them to Cork on the bus or to the various boarding institutions such as with the Jesuits at Rockwell College, Co. Tipperary (one of the finest rugby schools in Ireland where, it was said, the cream of the country were educated) or Blackrock College, Dublin.

Seán Hamilton hailed from Killarney; his father, a native of Limerick, settled there when he married a Kerry woman. Seán's mother, like many mothers at that time, saw education as the escape from poverty and a life of hardship and encouraged her three boys to work hard and become high achievers. Luckily, all three boys were brilliant. Bartholomew became a doctor and emigrated to Wales where he served as a respected G.P., married and had five daughters. His brother, Con, also became a teacher and settled in Cork with his wife, Eileen and family. Seán, having excelled in first level education, won a scholarship to second and third level. He attended University College Cork and graduated with a first class honours arts degree. It was there that he met the lovely Claire Maloney, a Cork city girl, who graduated with a commerce degree.

They were married in December 1946. Seán was an ambitious young man with a good head for business. He wanted to run his own school so, during his final year at university, he did some research and discovered that Bandon had no provision for the second level education of Catholic boys; the Protestant community were well served by an excellent grammar school. Bandon was a central town and students could be drawn from a radius of ten to twelve miles. It was a well populated area and so looked like a good place to start a school.

Seán, together with his business partner, Tom Cahill, a Limerick man, set up their first one-roomed school in 1940 above Hawkes Chemist Shop on South Main Street; Tom had the reputation of being a brilliant scholar and a dedicated teacher. The Bandon Secondary School or Mean Scoil na Banndan, opened its doors in its simple setting to nine students: Dan Lordan, that grand old gentleman from the 'Speckled Door' (An Doras Breac) near the Old Head of Kinsale; Joe Shorten, the only son of Ben Shorten, outfitters in the town; Seamus Scannell, who lived in Shannon Street and whose mother, Kit Roche, was a sister to Roche's the barbers; Fr Donie Canniffe, who lived in Bridge Street where his parents kept a shop, just around the corner from the school; John Quill, whose family was connected with Beamish and Crawford; Joe Hyde, whose family kept a pub in Shannon Street across from the West Cork Lane; Denis Driscoll, who went on to become a building contractor in the town; and the O'Brien brothers, TJ and Denis.

The two pioneers, Seán and Tom, did not have an easy time setting up their school. There was much opposition from the clergy, who felt that Farranferris would lose potential pupils and thereby result in fewer boys going on to the priesthood! At that time, only the sons of farmers and business people could afford to pursue a religious vocation. Seán and Tom's vision was to make education accessible to all or, if not to all, to as many as possible; there were still many people who could not afford the seven pounds and ten shillings per term which was the fee at that time.

Both men were general practitioners teaching all subjects.

Seán, who is remembered as a man with a perpetual smile on his face, cycled from Cork daily in those early days. Occasionally, on a very wet day, he might get a lift in a lorry or he might have to travel by train which of course was expensive, but his main mode of transport was his bicycle. Retired police inspector Joe Hyde – a regular contributor to the *Bandon Opinion* – remembers with great fondness the many games of handball he and Seán played at the Ball Alley behind Fulham's pub (now Nyhan's), after which Seán would get on his bicycle and return to Cork.

Tom, an older man, had lodgings in Bandon. Tom's efforts with the bicycle were not so successful. He learned to cycle late in life and bought a bike which, according to Joe Hyde, seemed to be always getting punctured, so he would regularly have to call on Denis O'Brien to mend it. Tom's bike seemed to be a great cause of amusement to those early scholars.

Eventually the school outgrew its rooms and in 1950 moved to the Still, the site of Allman's Distillery, into the former home and offices of the distillery manager. There were two big rooms and a storeroom on the ground floor and two large rooms and one smaller one on the first floor. The two teachers worked in three classrooms: the first and second years were together in one room; the two inter certificate classes had the second; and the smaller room housed the leaving certificate students. As the school grew, so did the need for more teachers. Paddy Tyers, the famous Cork goalie, joined the staff for a time, as did the legendary Con Houlihan, before he took up journalism and became the respected writer he is today. Other early staff members were Pat O'Sullivan, Fred Nagle and Frank Daly, all of whom are fondly remembered. Gerard Beirne from Co. Roscommon brought a whole new dimension to the school in the early 1950s as he was their first science teacher. Liam Deasy, who joined the school when it moved to the Still, remembers a great commotion on the day the boys spilled some mercury that went through the floorboards, causing quite a bit of damage.

It was a semi-gaelscoil and many of the subjects were taught through the medium of Irish. The boys did not have playing fields but were often entertained at lunch hour watching Seán Hamilton and Con Houlihan play handball. The students worked hard and got plenty of homework. When it came to the public examinations, they had to go to the Grammar School – now the site of the present Hamilton High School – to sit these exams.

When Tom Cahill left the school, the name changed to the Hamilton High School – the name it still enjoys today. In 1959, the school moved again, to its present site on the Laurel Walk. The Grammar School moved to Richmond House – to which new rooms had been added – in Old Chapel, in 1958. Bandon Grammar School is one of the oldest schools in Ireland, having been founded by the Earl of Cork, Richard Boyle, in 1641.

The current high school buildings comprise four Georgian houses built from 1810–12 and known as numbers one, two, three and four. These houses were the start of an intended square and had the prosperity of the town continued, the square would have been completed. The houses were originally dwellings and the pair fronting the road continued as such up to the 1960s. The corner house was first tenanted by 'Governor' Thomas Biggs, a woollen master, miller and provost (mayor) of the town in 1789, 1791 and 1793. After his death the Endowed (Grammar) School moved into this house. Number four was added to the school around 1830. The Bachelor Duke (6th) of Devonshire, patron of the school and owner of the walled town, himself stayed for some days at number two in 1812; in the nineteenth century this building also housed, consecutively, seven county inspectors of the RIC.

To this day the Hamilton High School is a school of the highest academic standards in the mode of the old style Grammar School. Many of the past pupils are now captains of industry and commerce. Most of Bandon's business men have been educated there: academics, priests, gardaí (the previous garda commissioner, Pat Byrne, attended the school for a time) and leaders in the world of education, medicine, the civil service, the legal profession (Judge Con Murphy is a past pupil) and banking.

Seán Hamilton will ever be revered in Bandon as the man who made it possible for its sons to have a brighter future and a chance in life; an opportunity which their fathers could not enjoy. He knew tragedy early on in his life when he lost his beloved wife Claire to cancer in 1973, leaving him with five young children to raise – Pádraig, his eldest son, Rhoda, Cliona, Ian and Brian, all of whom have excelled in their chosen careers – plus a school to run. He is remembered by the boys whom he taught as a strict teacher, but fair and good natured. He treated the boys well; and any student who had ability but could not afford the fees would not be turned away. He was a generous man.

In 1990, when the school was fifty years old, Seán reiterated the ethos of the school – Catholic, Gaelic and European:

'I would like to think at the end of fifty years that we, at the Hamilton High School, have succeeded to some extent in teaching valuable things outside the curriculum as well as inside – fidelity to your faith and fatherland and to your language, culture and games.'

7

The Farmer's Tale

'Go and get them for nawtin' then,' scowled Mossie Hurley, as he removed the bag of potatoes from the boot of the Bandon man's car. The man had come to buy a bag of potatoes from Mossie who had amicably placed them in the boot. When Mossie told him the price of the potatoes however, he had the temerity to say, 'That's too dear, sure spuds are for nawtin' now.' Hence Mossie's retort and the removal of the potatoes – the poor man had to leave 'potato-less'.

Mossie had inherited the farm from his father, Maurice Hurley, a man of great vision. He and his wife had made sure that their daughters, as well as their sons, had a good education: this in the days when the education of girls was considered a waste. Young Mossie was a tidy farmer and like many farmers living close to town, he sold vegetables to the natives. He hired some of the young lads from town during the holidays to thin beet, turnips or mangolds – a water-based vegetable used for fodder – and to pick potatoes. He also brought animals to the fair.

The fair day was a good day out, particularly if the animals were sold. Dealers had a very good eye for cattle. They could look at a beast and guess the weight to the nearest pound. They would then buy the cattle and either fatten them or sell them at a profit. At the fair the dealers employed tanglers or jobbers to hang around the cattle they had earmarked and prevent any other dealer butting in and paying a higher price. When the dealer and the farmer had fixed on a price the dealer would spit on his hand and the farmer would shake on it. They would then retire to the nearest pub – Hawkes, Tobin's, Deasy's or Driscoll's – to wet their whistles before returning home for the milking.

Farming was hard but healthy work and for the children it was a lot of fun. Phil was an adult, living in Wales, before she heard it called a 'business'. She had many happy memories of feeding calves, chickens and turkeys; collecting eggs from all the strange places where hens might have laid them as they wandered independently around the farmyard; going to the creamery with the churns in the donkey and cart; and getting up early to gather mushrooms for breakfast. Their Auntie Kitty would already have baked bread in the bastible for the breakfast before going out to milk the cows. Milk never tasted the same as that taken hot from the bucket. The greatest treat of all was helping her nan to make butter in the churn and then having the buttermilk with the home-grown potatoes for dinner, with a lovely knob of homemade butter on top.

Fetching water from the well was another of her jobs, but she would often spill half the bucket before getting back to the house. Years later she could remember the taste – it was so cold, clear and refreshing. It was better than champagne! Every afternoon she helped her Auntie Kitty take the tea out to her uncles Denny and Maurice, the workman, Eddie and her brother, Pat, who was considered old enough to help with the men's work in the fields. At haymaking time or during harvest time this was her favourite chore. There would be a gallon full of piping hot sweet tea and a basket of freshly made currant cake and brown bread with butter and jam. One of the lesser attractions of farming which she experienced was spending the night up in a dark shed with only a hurricane lantern for light and heat, while a sow was farrowing. Sometimes the sow would be brought into the kitchen beside the fire to prevent her from smothering the *bonamhs* (baby pigs).

Back then, hay was mowed by a horse and mower, then raked and put into haycocks to dry before being transported by horse and cart into the haggard under cover of the hay barn or shed. A contractor, with a reaper and binder attached to a tractor, would come to save the harvest; this was the forerunner of the combined harvester. Then they were ready for the fun part, the highlight of the year, the threshing, eagerly looked forward to by young and old. It was a day and night of real celebration. Each farmer in the parish helped the other and working parties moved from farm to farm until the whole parish was secure for the onset of winter.

The Bandon Co-op was set up by the farmers for the farmers in the early 1950s. All the big farmers around the Bandon area were members of this co-op and were the founding fathers of the Cork Co-op marts, Bandon being their first mart. When the mart was set up in 1957, Mossie, like other farmers, was apprehensive about the change; it was a brand new concept for many of them. They were used to cattle jobbers coming to the fair to buy cattle and everyone dealt in cash. Now, under the new system, the beasts had to be registered and the government would know exactly how much money was being made by the farmer. Nevertheless, the mart was a huge success.

Many of the cattle jobbers became drovers at the mart and could be seen daily herding large numbers of cattle through the eastern end of town to the railway holding yard. They often rushed into the Kilmichael Bar for a quick pint having deposited a herd of cows, ready for transportation. On mart days it was important that the people of Boyle Street and Shannon Street kept their doors shut as a dissident cow often wandered in and you can imagine the difficulty of trying to persuade a frightened bullock to reverse out of a narrow hallway. With the closure of the railway all this activity ceased and the drovers worked mainly on the mart site helping the animals to board the lorries which replaced the railway carriages.

Johnny Brien, one of the drovers, was a great favourite in the Kilmichael Bar. He told ghost stories and other tall tales to the amusement of all. That fatal day when the price of a pint of stout jumped from nine pence in old money to one and a penny in the budget, the shell shocked Johnny, with a moustache of good porter froth around his mouth, pronounced: 'I'll follow it to half a crown.'

Only fifty years later, the marts are now dying out and beasts are going straight to the meat factories. At one time Cork Co-operative had nine marts, based in Millstreet, Midleton, Fermoy, Skibbereen, Macroom, Mitchelstown, Dungarvan, Cahir and Bandon, but at least three of these have been closed in recent years and the others have been scaled down.

8

THE SAILOR'S TALE

I'll take you home again, Kathleen,
across the ocean wild and wide,
To where your heart has ever been,
since first you were my bonny bride.

The lofty baritone voice boomed out from the bar downstairs
and interrupted the 'long divisions' which Phil was coming to
grips with in her bedroom. Well to hell with homework, that
was Thomas' song – he must be home from the sea! Down
the stairs she flew and into the bar by the side door from the
hallway hoping to escape the landlady's sharp eye.

Thomas Crean was one of four children. Sadly, he was
too young to remember his father who had returned injured
from the First World War and died aged twenty-nine as a
result of his wounds. His mother struggled to feed and clothe
her children. Thomas and his brother, David, went to the

British legion office and signed up for the merchant navy in 1937, when he was eleven and David was thirteen. His older brother, John, had already joined the army. Only his sister, Peggy, remained at home. 'We had nothing,' said Thomas. 'What else could we do?' They were accepted and off they went to Hammersmith with fifty-six other young recruits, fifty of whom were Irish.

They lived on the training ship, *The Stork*, at Hammersmith on the Thames, where they received their general seamanship training as well as attending school in Hammersmith. They spent five years at the secondary school and each day, when they returned to the training ship at around 4 p.m., having showered and had tea, they attended classes in general seamanship. They learned all about knots and splices and how to handle cargo. Fitness on board ship was extremely important and they attended gymnastic classes three times a week. The daily routine was tough but Thomas enjoyed it. During the summer months the young boys rose at 6 a.m. and rowed on the river for two hours before going ashore to school.

Imagine Thomas' pride when he was chosen with twenty of his fellow cadets to march at the Armistice Day ceremony in the Albert Hall, carrying the merchant navy flag in the presence of his majesty, King George VI and Queen Elizabeth, the late queen mother.

For Thomas this was a splendid adventure; he worked hard and enjoyed himself. Before his seventeenth birthday, he was given the responsibility of steering a minesweeper up and down the Thames with three other boys. No navy personnel were available so the captain of the training ship had volunteered four of his best young men, Thomas amongst them. It was an exciting assignment but also a dangerous one as England was now at war.

Before he was eighteen, he travelled to Liverpool to join his first ship, *The Lech*, owned by the Polish British Steamship Company and managed by the Polish Steamship Agency. *The Lech* had been built in 1934 by Swan Hunter in Newcastle-upon-Tyne and had been strengthened for ice. The ship had been brought under the ministry of war transport (MOWT) and was now crewed by a variety of nationalities as the Polish crew had joined the free Polish navy.

Thomas made his first long sea voyage to Iceland where there was an American airbase. The boats travelled out in a convoy of about fifty troop ships, including *The Lech* and escorted by destroyers. The captains of these ships received their orders in sealed envelopes which were not to be opened until they were far out in the Atlantic. The use of wirelesses was forbidden during wartime as it was easy for submarines to pick up such information. A signalling system called sema-phore – an alphabet signalling system based on the waving of a pair of hand-held flags in a particular pattern – was used by day and Aldus lamps were used by night. The young men had learned these communication skills while aboard *The Stork*.

The convoy were to split at Iceland where *The Lech* docked

and the remainder would continue on to Russia. Their cargo was ammunition for the army. When it was unloaded, they travelled around the Icelandic fjords picking up salted fish and dried cod to bring back to England before returning to Reykjavik to meet their convoy and return home to Liverpool. There were German submarines all around the Atlantic and the ships had to zig-zag to avoid them, but, as Thomas said: 'You don't see any danger when you're young.'

The Lech did a few more trips to Iceland and back before departing for the Mediterranean in 1943 where it remained for sixteen months, carrying troops on the top deck and stores and ammunition on the lower decks, to and from the various ports on the Mediterranean. Meanwhile, Thomas' brother, David, was on a troop ship. Happily, the brothers met at Port Said in 1944. 'It was a million to one chance,' said Thomas. 'When the ship was going down the Suez Canal, I got a rowing boat and went across to see him. We were so delighted to see each other and we spent a few pleasant hours together.'

Conditions were tough on the troop ships. The men slept in hammocks, ten to a room. They assembled on deck for physical exercise and were kept busy throughout each voyage. One of their missions was to transport a regiment of Ghurkhas from Naples around to Bari on the Adriatic coast. The Ghurkhas from Nepal had served the British crown since 1815. At the end of the Anglo–Nepali war of 1812–15, the British East India Company were so impressed by the bravery and fighting skills of the Nepali soldiers that they raised the first regiment of Ghurkhas. When India became independent in 1947, four Ghurkha regiments transferred to the British army, but remained based in the Far East. Their preferred weapon of war was the khukuri, a knife which every Nepali boy is likely to own before the age of five, thus acquiring great skill in its use. The khukuri is a tool with a variety of uses: hunting, chopping wood, cutting food and clearing a jungle. The Ghurkha soldier keeps his khukuri as he keeps his honour, 'bright and keen'. As a weapon of war it struck fear into the hearts of the Germans.

At the end of the war there were more ships than men which gave experienced sailors like Thomas a choice. He joined the Cardiff pool of seamen and signed on a cargo ship travelling from Germany to Galveston in very difficult weather conditions. The engine stopped five times on the outward journey but eventually limped into Galveston where it was repaired. On the homeward journey it broke down three times before it docked at Newcastle-upon-Tyne and was put in dry dock for repair. Thomas laughed off any talk of being frightened, 'I take life as it comes,' was his philosophical reply.

Following this trip Thomas worked on *The Wave Premiere*, a fleet auxiliary tanker, which fuelled aircraft carriers and destroyers.

Having done a few trips around Britain in coasters, as small cargo ships were called, Thomas joined the Orient line in 1949 and was assigned to the *Ormond*, a 28,000 ton liner. This was the first passenger ship of the Orient line to transport emigrants to Australia under the £10 scheme. The emigrants were dropped off at Freemantle, Adelaide, Melbourne, Brisbane and Sydney and were called '£10 Pommies' by the Australians.

Thomas fell in love with the beautiful Maureen Looney and on 10 June 1952, they were married. It was a wonderful day – a typical Bandon wedding, much singing, dancing and drinking. Thomas and his great friend Corney Looney, as well as being related through drink, were now related through marriage. Having worked in England before she was married, Maureen now stayed in Bandon where both their boys were born: Seán, who sadly died of motor-neuron disease in 1998 and Neil, who still lives in the family home with his wife and family. Of course, after his marriage, Tom hated leaving home since he would be away at least six months at a time. Later, with improved technology, his work schedule was reduced to four and a half months, which provided him with the opportunity of spending six weeks at home.

It was not uncommon in those days to carry cargo on passenger ships. Thomas worked on a variety of ships for Orient until he joined the *Canberra* – a 45,000 ton luxury liner with a capacity to carry 1,641 passengers. It was known as the Great White Whale and took its passengers on world cruises. On 2 April 1982, the liner was requisitioned for use in the Falklands' War, refitted to carry troops and was used as a hospital ship. Thankfully, it was returned to its owners later the same year. There are no big jetties in Stanley, so the troops had to be brought ashore by helicopter. The helicopters landed in the Main Street, where there were only one or two shops and a canteen for the servicemen. Thomas travelled to the Falklands on board the *Uganda*, another P&O ship which had been requisitioned by the army and used as a hospital ship. Once again this quiet, fun loving Bandon man was involved in conflict.

In 1973, as he approached the beautiful island of Mauritius, Thomas received a cable aboard the *Canberra* asking him to join a new ship which the company had bought. He enjoyed two weeks in Bandon with his family before flying to Galveston to collect the *Pacific Princess* and bring her to Los Angeles.

Thomas spoke highly of the company which employed him for thirty-eight years: the Peninsular and Orient Steam and Navigational Company, known as the P&O line. In 1837, the company had started a service to Spain and Portugal carrying mail for the government; it was the first overseas mail contract given to commercial operators. In 1840, mail was transported to Egypt and India, thereby adding 'Oriental' to the company title. When the Suez Canal opened in 1869, P&O ran services through to the Far East and Australia. Tickets were stamped P.O.S.H., 'Port out, Starboard home', providing passengers with the cooler side of the ship, best protected from the glare of the sun on the sea in the days before air-conditioning – and so the word 'posh' entered the English language! During the First World War the company lost half a million tons of shipping. In 1939, they had 2,000,000 tons of shipping, but again they lost half of it during the Second World War. The company expanded into tanker and cargo ships during the 1950s.

In 1984, Thomas had the great pleasure of meeting Princess Diana when she launched *The Royal Princess*. Afterwards, princess and sailor had a drink and an informal chat. He was very impressed by her friendliness and cordiality. The construction of *The Royal Princess* made a deep impression on Thomas. The ship was built under cover in Helsinki. Because of its length, it had been built in two halves. This was a new experience for him as ships had always been built out in the open. He stayed in Helsinki for four months while the ship was being prepared for sea and then proudly sailed her back to Southampton for her launch voyage and naming.

In his forty-five years at sea, Thomas saw some fantastic sights – sights which many of us only dream about. He had sailed under the Sydney Harbour Bridge, witnessed amazing sunrises and sunsets, as well as the indescribable aurora borealis and travelled under the night sky in the Indian Ocean! He learned the different customs and a lot about the culture of the various countries he visited during his long seafaring career. He was also aware of some of the degradation suffered by people, mainly in the southern hemisphere, where poverty and corrupt governments make the lives of the ordinary people miserable. One of the sights which most disturbed him was that of young girls being sold into prostitution in Bombay. He also met people from his home town in various countries around the world, some in Australia and some in New Zealand. One of the men whom he met could never come home because of an illness he had contracted during the First World War. This illness prevented him from flying or travelling by sea. Others had become political exiles through their involvement in paramilitary activities and were too frightened to come home for fear of punishment.

Every January, Thomas did a world trip. He served on the now famous *Oriana* – the last ship of the Orient line before its amalgamation with P&O. The *Oriana* was later sold to the Chinese and sadly, during a typhoon in July 2004, it was dashed against the harbour walls causing damage beyond repair. Being no longer seaworthy, it was sent to the breakers' yard. Many seafarers were saddened by the demise of this beautiful luxury liner with its magnificent furnishings and ornamentation.

Thomas was aboard the *Canberra* in January 1987 during the famous rescue of the Jones family off the coast of Mexico. Near the end of their five-year round the world voyage, a British family from Sussex were heading for Acapulco when their thirty-five foot ketch broke up in high seas. They got on their life raft where they spent eighteen hours before being spotted by a Korean ship which radioed the *Canberra* for help.

For a number of years Thomas worked on the *Empire Thackeray* doing the paper run (printing paper) from Newfoundland to Washington and was on the ship when it sank off Newfoundland:

Winter was coming; we came to Halifax and decided to do another trip. We were travelling through a narrow passage in a Force 12 gale. It was a dirty night and I was on the 12 to 4 watch. I came off at 4 a.m., breakfasted, showered and turned in. I had one leg in the bed when I heard the bang; we had hit a rock. The alarm went off and we all assembled on the bridge. Suddenly she came to a dead stop. We waited until it was light to see what had happened. We were home and dry. We couldn't get off, but we could see land as we neared a cliff. We were a crew of 25. I was let down the hatch in the bosun's chair to assess the damage. There were five rocks sticking up in different positions throughout the hull. The locals from the village of Lumsden North came with food and clothes for us. They put us up in their homes where they really looked after us. They warmed a brick in the fire, wrapped it in a blanket and put it in the bed to keep us warm. They were lovely people, kind and generous. We lived on a diet of fresh fish. We spent a week there before setting off on sleighs to the nearest station, an eight day journey away. The local men carried two of us on each sleigh which was pulled by the huskies – it was brilliant! We travelled over rough, open country covered with snow and forests until we reached St John's. We crossed on the ferry from St John's to Halifax where we stayed in a hotel until we were picked up by the *Mauritania* and brought home to Southampton.

Thomas' brother, David, came ashore after the war, married and worked on the docks in Liverpool where he still lives. His brother, John, who died some years ago, had a distinguished career in the army. While David was working on the troop ships, picking up wounded soldiers and taking them to field hospitals, imagine his surprise on one occasion in Naples when he picked up a stretcher on which lay his brother, John, who had been wounded in action.

He was in the Falkland Islands when his mother died and the speed with which he got home bears testament to the efficiency of the company for which he worked. He travelled by helicopter to the mainland, boarded an army plane to Brize Norton air force base, was taken by car to Heathrow airport and flew home. On another occasion he was on his way to Mexico when he got news of his beloved Maureen's illness. Within a day, having been flown from Acapulco, he was by her side.

Thomas was the idol of the children of Foxes Street Cross. It was difficult to imagine the kind of work he did, especially in the days before television. They all knew the type of labour undertaken by those employed in breweries and the timber yard, but Thomas' work was a mystery to them. He was a big handsome man with a huge voice and a laugh which came all the way up from his toes. They loved how he walked in that side-to-side gait peculiar to sailors and he always had time for them.

In 1987, after a long and loyal service, Thomas bade farewell to the sea and returned to his native Bandon. He had served as bosun for twenty-five years. At the time he retired he was in charge of a crew of thirty-five men. His sense of humour, no doubt, was of great advantage to him in getting the best out of the men. To mark his retirement, wonderful ceremonies took place in Southampton where he was wined and dined for five days and given a carriage clock, a hefty cheque and a pension for life.

9

THE DANCER'S TALE

The main musical personality of Bandon from the 1920s to the 1950s was Lizzy May Cohalan, mother of Mickey the bandleader. She organised numerous concerts and shows with her Green Dramatic Troupe and was at the hub of town entertainment for over fifty years.

Lizzy May was the only surviving daughter of John and Kate Walsh who had a coach factory at the end of Church Drive on the New Road, where Bolster's Funeral Home is now situated. John did most of the work in the church: the pedestals on which saints Bridget and Patrick stand were skilfully carved by him; and the pulpit, a beautifully ornate piece of furniture – removed during recent refurbishment and now housed in a storeroom off Warner's Lane – is the handiwork of him and his men. To the men's and the canon's amusement he was the first to speak from that pulpit: in a unique version of St Paul's letter to the Colossians, he announced that Paul said, 'The canon should go down to Keohane's pub and stand a round of drinks to John Walsh and his men!' He was also a very good musician – the cornet was his instrument.

Kate made and sold sweets and so was a very popular lady with the children of the town. Her granddaughter, Celia O'Brien, vividly remembered the beautiful smell around the house of maple syrup and other mouth-watering ingredients for her bull's eyes and other hard sweets. Unfortunately the recipes died with Kate.

John and Kate Walsh had a sad start in life. In those days of high infant mortality all their sons died of childhood illnesses. As they returned from the burial of their last boy, they wondered how they could possibly go back to such an empty and lonely house. Shortly afterwards, in 1895, they were blessed with a precious baby girl – Lizzy May. Lizzy May had two sisters but both died at a young age. She grew up to become a beautiful young woman with music in her soul. Her parents, recognising her enormous talent, sent her to piano and dancing lessons from a young age. On one occasion the canon visited her primary school, the Presentation Convent, to find Lizzy May out on the corridor in punishment.

'What are you doing here, Lizzy May?' he asked.

'I didn't know my Irish, canon,' she replied.

He took her by the hand and returned her to class saying to her teacher, 'Sure sister, all her Irish is in her feet.'

Lizzy May won the Munster Step-Dancing Championship in 1913, dancing the three-hand reel. She was the youngest member of the Bandon Musical Society which was directed by Patrick Murphy, principal of St Fintan's School. Her stage debut came at the Allin Institute when she was ten years old and she was barely in her teens when she played the title role in *Lily of Killarney*. She made her final appearance on the same stage fifty-three years later when she was sixty-three and very ill. She always exhibited that wonderful showbiz spirit – the show must go on, no matter what. The Coholan School of Dancing was set up in the 1920s. Lizzy May taught singing, modern dance and drama, as well as Irish Step Dancing. Her 'shows' were a main feature of the town's life during the 1920s, 1930s, 1940s and 1950s. Her troupe was performing in a St Patrick's night concert and she had to be there for them. She returned to her sick bed suffering from pneumonia and died on 21 March 1958. Her son, Anthony, recalled that his band had been booked to play in Kerry on that St Patrick's night and there was some doubt as to whether they could attend because of his mother's illness. They did go and on their return he recalls Do-Do Downing – that other musical genius from Bandon – going up to visit his mother when she was very weak.

Lizzy May experienced hard times but they never bore her down; she would continue to sit at her piano and play her favourite tunes. Often the cups and saucers would be pushed aside, the sewing machine would be brought out and she would spend the evening making costumes. Of course, as her children grew older, they were a great help to her and were able to assist with the step dancing classes, teaching the beginners and accompanying the more advanced dancers on the piano.

Lizzy May married the handsome Michael Cohalan from Carrigdangan, Kilmichael – a relative of the Most Reverend Daniel Cohalan, bishop of Cork and Canon Jeremiah Cohalan, who served in Bandon. The family name was actually Cahalane but when the bishop went to Rome as a clerical student, the Italians could not pronounce Cahalane so he became Cohalan and all the family adopted this variation of the name. Michael was one of fifteen children. Being a special favourite of his mother she sent him off to Dublin to train as a draper in one of the big shops. He eventually moved back to Cork where he worked in Leaders drapery in North Main Street. He joined the Cork Pipers Club – a happy coincidence which was responsible for his meeting with Lizzy May. He moved to a drapery in Bandon when they married but it was burned down by the black and tans during the Troubles.

Being a good gardener he then went to work for the canon and remained there until his death. They had eight children, five girls and three boys. Michael was a very good upholsterer and made beautiful toys for his children; Celia remembers a particularly lovely rocking horse he made for Anthony and John. He helped the children with their homework and taught them their prayers. It was a happy and creative household. Sadly, their eldest son, John, died in 1947 of meningitis when he was sixteen years old. The other seven children all inherited their mother's musical and dancing talent. Mickey was a reluctant step dancer, preferring gymnastics, but could be persuaded to take part in a three- or four-hand reel if they were short. He later became a very skilled ballroom dancer.

At *feiseanna* and competitions throughout the county the Cohalan School of Dancing usually swept the board. Lizzy May's dancers seemed to have had that extra 'something' which gave them the edge over other schools of dancing.

Lizzy May was a true professional and an exceptional lady, excelling in all areas of stagecraft: she wrote her own scripts, produced and directed the musicals, designed and made the costumes and sets, did the lighting as well as the choreography and the musical accompaniment. Nowadays, a whole team of people is needed to put on a show. She has been compared to Maureen Potter, with her quick wit, talent for satire and gift for singing, dancing, acting and playing music. During the era of the silent movies she played the piano in the cinema to accompany such movie stars as Charlie Chaplin, Greta Garbo and other heroes of the silent screen.

She was a champion Irish dancer and her five daughters all followed in her footsteps, thereby promoting Irish culture and dance: Noreen, in Macroom; Mercy, in Ballineen; Cullie, in north London; Celia, in Bandon; and Pat, also in London, where she danced for the Irish ambassador at the Mansion House (the home of London's lord mayor) and then later in Kent. Like their mother they also trained world class dancers. Five of Lizzy May's granddaughters are now teaching dancing and three are teaching music. Lizzy May's sons were very talented musicians: Mickey played the piano accordion, the piano and any other instrument he happened to pick up; and Anthony, a multi-talented musician, mainly played the saxophone.

Dance is one of our oldest forms of expression and is natural to all of us. How often do we see little children skipping and dancing playfully, reflecting the great cosmic dance which brought our planet into being? Unfortunately many become so inhibited as they grow up that they seem to forget how to dance. Little is known about the dance of the early Celts or Gaels, but the wonderful Celtic designs are evident in the costumes worn by Irish step dancers to this day. These intricate geometric patterns, knot work and the continuous lines have been produced in Ireland since the eighth century and are taken from the illuminated manuscripts of the time. Happily we can still see one of the great masterpieces of this period, the wonderful Book of Kells, on view in Trinity College, Dublin.

The *feiseanna* also date back to this period when they were a combination of trade fair, political gathering and cultural event with music, sport, storytelling and craft. Over a period of time the cultural events began to dominate *feiseanna* and they now consist of music, drama and dance. The first mention of step dancing appears to be in the mid fifteenth century, when the *rince fada*, the long dance, is mentioned, as are jigs, which were likely to have been done in a group, trenchmores, a big free form country type dance and sword dances. During the

Penal times traditional Irish culture was practised in secret. This period of severe repression lasted for over a hundred years which explains some of the secrecy surrounding the teaching of step dancing. Certainly we are delighted to know that during this most difficult time the Irish continued to keep their culture alive in spite of the state and church which frequently condemned the 'frenzy' of the dance.

Dance masters appeared about 1750 and that tradition, to which Lizzy May belongs, continues to this day. The teachers are now mainly female but in those days the dance master would come to a village and stay about six weeks, lodging with a hospitable family who considered it an honour to accommodate him. He would teach Irish dancing in kitchens, barns, sheds, at crossroads and at the hedge school. The jig and reel were the first dances to be taught. Each dance master had a repertoire of dance steps and he also created new steps; eight bars of music are called a step, which is the origin of the term 'step dancing'. The cake dance became popular in the 1800s: a cake would be placed on a stand in the centre of a field as a prize for the best dancer and the winner would 'take the cake'. Attempts by the parish priests to suppress dancing thankfully failed. The Gaelic League was formed in 1893 to revive the practice of Irish culture. In 1929, the Irish Dancing Commission was founded to establish rules regarding teaching, judging and competitions. Irish dancing is now taught all over the world and is enjoying a renaissance.

A few theories have been put forward as to the stiff upper

body of the step dancers. One relates to the 'stage' which might be a barrel, a table top or a half door and would have left little room for hand movements. Another theory has to do with the venue: the dances were often performed in pubs or in barns where space was limited and movement of the arms might be hazardous to both dancer and audience. The final theory is that the movement of the arms would take the attention from the intricacies of the footwork which were so quick and skilful. Lizzy May was at the forefront of Irish dancing in Co. Cork. She was a free spirit – an Isadora Duncan – who promoted free movement and the beauty of the human body in its myriad of movements. She instinctively knew that the more stylised Irish dance would evolve into the much freer art form of today. This 'Lady of the Dance' would have revelled in the spectacle of *Riverdance* and *Lord of the Dance*.

Generations of young people in Bandon can rejoice that Lizzy May lived there and shared her talent and enthusiasm with them. Had she been born in Dublin or London there is no doubt but that she would have been a professional performer. She loved children and they loved her; she could get the best out of them. She never worried about money and if children could not pay for their dancing lessons, she would not turn them away. She has been loved by all who knew her and has become a folk heroine to those who were not so lucky, but who have heard from their parents and grandparents the stories of her talent, energy and charisma.

10

THE RUGBY PLAYERS' TALE

Tommy Canniffe is best remembered for his fleet footed rendering of 'Mexico' in the Kilmichael Bar: everybody had to stand well back and give him enough space to demonstrate his Fred Astaire-like dancing skills. In Tommy's case, the next song would always be a dance! But it was on the rugby field that he really exhibited his fancy footwork.

Tommy was born in number 13, Foxes Street, where he still lives. His father, who fought in the First World War and thankfully survived, was a member of the much acclaimed Bandon Workingmen's Fife and Drum band. When Tommy was only five or six years old unemployment forced his father to emigrate to England. Tommy was the second youngest of six children, all of whom emigrated, some to America and some to England. His sister, Ann, returned from London to marry Dan Riordan.

Like so many young boys of his time Tommy had to help

support the family at a young age. His schooling ended in Warner's Lane School at the age of fourteen when he went to work at the cinema as an usher. He had also a variety of other jobs. He worked for Jeffers', assisting the van driver with his deliveries. In the 1950s Jeffers' was one of Bandon's largest enterprises, comprising a bakery, a coffee shop, a mill and a shop with an extensive range of groceries. He also joined the potato-picking and vegetable-thinning crews of young men who were collected from Bandon bridge in horses and carts or tractors. All that farm work had to be done by hand in those days and it was back-breaking work. In 1952, Tommy got a lucky break, a job with the West Cork Bottling Company travelling the countryside delivering Murphy's stout and minerals to the pubs of West Cork. When it closed in 1978 he was transferred to the Kinsale Road Bottling Company, a subsidiary of Murphy's brewery. Unfortunately, three years later, the bottling section was closed and he was made redundant.

In 1952, he started to play rugby. He played for Bandon for sixteen seasons.

People have been playing ball with their feet for thousands of years but it took the English to regularise it in 1863. Until then there were no rules so anything was possible: the only two fouls were murder and manslaughter, otherwise a player could kick, thump or punch to his heart's content. The game, which could last for several days, moved through fields and villages wreaking havoc on all sides. Successive governments worldwide tried to ban the game but failed. Finally, the teachers at England's public schools thought it was a good character-building exercise and set about applying some rules. In 1863, there was a parting of the ways when Rugby public school favoured handling the ball and running with it and also preferred the rougher game; hence we have association football and rugby football.

Rugby was first played in Ireland at Trinity College, Dublin, in 1854, without the public school rules. Each college seemed to have its own rules. It was introduced into south Munster by graduates from that prestigious college who came to teach or practise law in Cork, Midleton and Bandon. The students of Queen's College Cork, now University College Cork, also played.

Frank Levis, a young lawyer who lived in Watergate Street, seems to have been the driving force behind the foundation of the Bandon rugby club. A common misperception is that the club was founded by the British army garrison but in fact no member of the army either played with, or became involved in the administration of the club. By the 1880s Bandon had regular games with Cork County, Cork Bankers and Queen's College. The Bandon Grammar School also had a rugby team.

Rugby football was the only form of organised football at this time in the area. Association football is mentioned in sports' reports in 1893, ten years later and Gaelic football appeared following the founding of the GAA in 1884, so any mention of football in the press and other literature of the nineteenth century refers to rugby. By 1882, the rugby club was the centre of social life in Bandon. As the number of teams multiplied the game became more organised and the rules more formalised.

The political situation in Ireland at the turn of the century was volatile and caused problems for these fledgling clubs. Nationalist feelings were running high and ruthless murders were not uncommon. Unfortunately these disturbing events spilled over onto sporting activities. The GAA was promoting Irish games and forbidding its members to play 'foreign' games under its famous 'Rule 27' which was abolished in 1971. Rugby was considered a foreign game, having originated in England. Thankfully, Bandon retained an amicable relationship between both sports.

The Troubles at home and the outbreak of the First World War put a stop to all sporting activities in the early part of the nineteenth century. Local solicitor, Jim Neville, set about re-organising the rugby club in the mid 1920s. He succeeded in getting many of the young men of the town involved. Families associated with rugby in Bandon at this time were: the Phelans, business people in the town; the Polands, of musical fame; the Seamans, the Nagles and the O'Neills. Billy O'Neill was an all round sportsman who played rugby, football and hurling, as well as hunting and fishing. No wonder his sons Raymond, Barry and Brendan went on to distinguish themselves on the playing fields of Bandon. The Quills and the Walshes, both names associated with Beamish's brewery and the Brennans, of Mill and West Cork Bottling Company fame, were also at the forefront of rugby in the town. The Bandon team of the 1920s and early 1930s was hard to beat.

The Economic War in the early 1930s, with its attendant hardships of emigration and unemployment, took its toll on the local rugby club which sadly closed. Many of the older players retired and some of the remaining younger men joined Cork clubs and played senior rugby.

In 1937/38 a group of young men who had never played rugby set about reviving the club, using the Devonshire Arms Hotel as its base. Mr McCutcheon, headmaster of the Grammar School, agreed to become the club's president and this greatly encouraged these young men. T.D. Jones, who had never played rugby, became secretary. When Tim Quill, a veteran of the old team, joined them, their confidence grew. The proceeds from a dress dance in the Devon and a concert in the town hall enabled the fledgling club to buy a ball and a set of jerseys. The game now moved to Morgan's field behind Kilbrogan cemetery. Later, Paddy Murphy of Monarone, a player and supporter of rugby, put a field at the disposal of the new club. For bureaucratic reasons the new club became known as the Bandon Harlequins.

During the Second World War the club once again went into decline, but there was another revival in 1946. It really should have been called the Phoenix Club because it had so many resurrections from the ashes. It is a tribute to the courage and stamina of those determined men who kept the sport alive in the town. The revival of the broadcasting of international games did much to help the game; young boys caught the excitement of the game from the radio commentators and wanted to play. The first rugby dance was held on 3 January 1951 in the Devon and was so popular that it became an annual event in Bandon's social calendar. The famous Dixieland Showband made their debut at a rugby club dance held at Inchydoney.

Six years after this final revival Tommy started to play and he so enhanced the team that he has become a legend. Although he was small in stature, he was an excellent scrum half who made many a mediocre fly half look good. He was dynamite on the pitch. As a game against a city side was drawing to a close, he whipped out a stray pass from the base of the scrum. The opposition stormed up to boot the ball to safety only to discover that it was a dry cow turd and the ball was nestling safely on Tommy's foot – Bandon scored.

Tommy tells some great stories about the Welsh teams who visited during the Easter weekends. At the dinners held in their honour there was some excellent rugby and many convivial evenings of drinking and rugby talk with some spectacular singing thrown in. Ogmore Vale and Briton Ferry are two of the teams well remembered by the Bandon club, especially Briton Ferry who were particularly destructive, returning to Wales with a complete bathroom suite as a memento of their visit to West Cork! No doubt the hoteliers in the town did not look forward to these weekends of alarmingly high spirits.

With Tommy wearing the blue number nine, the Bandon team of the early 1960s was fantastic. He played on the minor team in 1954 and captained the minor team in 1955 after which he went on to junior league. He was captain again in 1957 and in 1965. He was on the teams which won the county cup in 1959 and 1961. During the O'Neill cup game in the 1965/66 season, Tommy had to be taken off the field with a head injury, but his team seemed to have gained inspiration from the setback and went on to win the cup.

The first trophy won by Bandon Rugby Club was in 1886: the Munster Senior Challenge Cup. The last trophies of the twentieth century were won by the under-twelve team: the South Munster Plate, the West Cork Cup and the Highfield Festival Plate. This certainly bodes well for the future of rugby in Bandon.

Tommy was forced to retire from the game he loved because of a knee injury. In 1982, he had the great honour of being invited back to join his team mates in the 'Golden Oldies' match which was celebrating the opening of the new rugby grounds in Old Chapel. He managed to play for the entire game. The friendships Tommy formed, north, south east and west, during his rugby playing career have endured long after the game. He recalls a game at Castleisland in the 1950s when the water mains in the town had burst and the team had to wash with Cidona after the game!

Philomena has fond memories of the day when Tommy and his friend Barry Ellis visited her at the Convent of Mercy in

Kinsale. They boarded the bus from Bandon, had a drink in one of the local hostelries and made their way up the steep hill to the convent. As they were about to ring the doorbell, they realised they hadn't brought a gift. Off they went down the hill, bought a box of chocolates and arrived back at the convent door puffing and panting having negotiated the Middle Hill twice. They were admitted by Sr Angela, the portress, who showed them into the parlour to await Phil's arrival. Phil was amused to see her two uncomfortable friends balancing on the end of their chairs, speaking in whispers and trying not to move as their shoes made too much noise on the tiled and wooden floors. Tea arrived with some of Sr Angela's special brown bread and chocolate cake which the boys enjoyed. However, they still seemed to be somewhat uncomfortable.

Eventually they confided to Phil that they were desperate for a smoke. To relieve the situation an ashtray was found and they lit up and relaxed. The convent parlour was certainly a forbidding setting for the two friends but the trouble they had taken to visit placed them firmly close to Phil's heart. These boys, whom she has known all her life, had always been ready to help her. When she was alone in the KB it was this duo who checked the outside toilet and the back yard and made sure the bar was empty before they left at night.

Tommy still enjoys a pint and a chat in the KB – even a sing-song. He can still perform 'Mexico' – that popular rock and roll song written by Mitchell Torok (better known as Mexican Joe) in 1956 when it spent sixteen weeks in the charts – or 'My Lily of the Lamplight'. He is still smiling, helping people and visiting the older folk in the Cottage Hospital. He is possibly the only person still living in Foxes Street who has been born there. He has seen many changes, particularly in the KB, but to the family who lived there from 1942 to 1975 he is still the greatest. Phil, lying in her sick bed above the bar was often entertained by Tommy's melodious tones wafting up the stairs, sometimes to the amusement of the local doctor on a visit to her:

Down in Mexico, at each high noon
Siesta is the thing.
You can find me sleepin' out in the shade
While the birds softly sing.
But from the radio, there comes a US show
And the disc-jockey's playin' the blues.
Before they know what's happened
They're up and clappin'
To the tune of the blue suede shoes.

11

THE DOCTOR'S TALE

Dr Eugene (Nudge) Callanan is best summed up by the final stanza of 'If' by Rudyard Kipling:

> If you can talk with crowds and keep your virtue,
> Or walk with Kings – nor lose the common touch,
> If neither foes nor loving friends can hurt you,
> If all men count with you, but none too much;
> If you can fill the unforgiving minute
> With sixty seconds' worth of distance run,
> Yours is the Earth and everything that's in it,
> And – which is more – you'll be a Man, my son!

And what a man – he was known, loved and respected by generations of Bandonians. His easy manner and ready wit made him welcome in any company. Everybody felt comfortable and at ease with him.

Eugene was born on 14 November 1898 in Magazine Road, the Lough parish, in Cork. His father was secretary to Cork County Council – known as the county manager today. One of ten children, he received his primary education at Glasheen national school, from where he graduated to the North Monastery school and from there to UCC to pursue his medical studies.

While a student, he joined the university branch of the IRA and together with his friend, Peter Kearney, interrupted his studies to join Tom Barry's flying column. He became an officer with the column and assistant medical officer to Dr Con Lucey. One day during the War of Independence he was hit on the hip by a bullet. He made his way across fields to a farm where he was taken care of in an outhouse. He spent a few days resting at Buttimer's farm in Gurranreigh – the landlady' home – until he was fit enough to rejoin the column. The wound he received in this incident left him with a limp. Sometime later he had a lucky escape at the Crossbarry ambush when a grenade rebounded off a tree and fell at his feet – it did not explode.

He returned to university after the truce, resumed his studies and qualified as a doctor. His first appointment was as public health doctor at Innishannon. While there, he played on the Valley Rovers hurling and football teams. Later he moved to Bandon where he served the community with dedication for over fifty years. His commitment to his patients knew no bounds.

As well as reaching academic heights he also excelled on the sports field, playing both football and hurling for his college. He won three Fitzgibbon medals and three Sigerston Cup medals. On leaving university, he played with Collegians, Cork and Munster, winning a Railway Cup medal in 1926 and a Munster Senior football medal in 1928. It was his prowess on the sporting field that earned him the name 'Nudge': he could sneak up at any moment and nudge the ball away from his opponent. In later life he took up golf and was a regular player at the Bandon Club, where he served as captain in 1947, president in 1953, 1969 and 1976 and was later made an honorary life member.

Greyhound racing was another passion of the good doctor. He came to that sport from the inspiration of his brother Arthur, a vet who specialised in greyhounds. Arthur Callanan was manager of the White City racing track in London, but returned to Ireland when the Second World War broke out. He rose to fame through his connection with the famous greyhound, Mick Miller, which stands embalmed in the museum at Tring, in Hertfordshire. The dog was named after the Mick Miller who had worked at the presbytery where the dog was born and who had looked after him as a puppy. The dog, part of a litter of twelve, was bred by Fr Brophy. Despite the care he received, Mick the Miller developed distemper before his first birthday. There were no vaccines in 1920s Ireland to combat this disease but Fr Brophy was determined to keep the dog alive. He took him to Arthur who was manager of

Shelbourne Park at the time. Even though the dog was frail, Arthur thought he could save him so he asked the priest to leave the dog with him. Indeed he did save the dog and returned him to his owner in good health several months later.

In April 1928 the almost two-year-old Mick the Miller made his racing debut. He was a winner from the very beginning, taking part in twenty races in Ireland and winning fifteen of them. His trainer, Mick Horan, knew he had a great dog. Accordingly he persuaded Fr Brophy it was time for the big league, so Mick the Miller was taken to England in 1929 to enter for the English Derby. He had his first trial at the White City and he was a sensation. He was put in as favourite to win the derby. Everybody wanted to buy the dog so he was auctioned on the terrace steps immediately after the successful trial. He was sold for 800 guineas to a London bookmaker. His success on the race tracks of England is legendary but he would not even have made it to his first birthday except for the loving care he received from the talented vet, Arthur Callanan. Arthur sadly died at the young age of fifty and Dr Nudge kept his interest in greyhounds in memory of his beloved brother.

Dr Callanan had many winners himself and was a regular attendee at the track on Western Road as well as at coursing events throughout Munster on miserable winter days. Johnny 'next door' to the KB used to train dogs for various greyhound owners including the good doctor. As a boy, Phil's brother,

Frank, would have to rise at dawn to walk these dogs and give them a good run in the Cottage Hospital field (before Ardan was built) or up to the four crosses, a nice little amble before breakfast. Johnny always had a dog or two in residence and on days when Frank was not available these dogs would race around the KB field. Most of Dr Callanan's dogs had the prefix Kilbrogan in front of their names – Kilbrogan Lad, Kilbrogan Boy – after Kilbrogan House, the Callanan family home, a beautiful Georgian House with a walled garden. Phil remembers at least one exception however, his famous dog Friends Everywhere, a metaphor for the doctor himself.

Eugene married the lovely Girlie O'Sullivan from Innishannon in 1930; he had met Girlie during his stint as medical officer at Innishannon. They had six children, four girls and two boys. Their daughter, Margaret Shorten, still lives in Bandon where she is active in the local community. Another daughter, Catherine Field, has made quite a name for herself in amateur dramatics in Skibbereen where she is a skilled producer of the local dramatic society's productions. Elizabeth, a physiotherapist, lives in Kilkenny, while their daughter Ann emigrated to Australia. The two boys, John and Eugene, both had successful dental practices in England from which they are now retired. Eugene has returned to West Cork where he is enjoying the craic.

Dr Callanan delivered generations of Bandonian babies including the six children for whom the KB was home. He never lost his sense of awe and wonder at the miracle of birth and stories abound about his special skills in gynaecology. It has been said that his hands were given a special blessing at Lourdes, that he always knelt and prayed after a safe delivery and that he put a half crown in the Martin de Porres box in St Philomena's nursing home. Whatever the truth of these stories, he did acknowledge the presence of a higher power in the great mysteries of life and death.

In those days most babies were born at home and the doctor was assisted by the wonderful midwife Mary Crowley who lived in South Main Street. She kept all her prodigies from becoming too 'uppity' by calling out to anybody who ignored her: 'When did you become so important? Sure you would not be here at all only for me.' She was a gracious lady who was much loved in the town.

Back then, pregnant women didn't have access to much information and Dr Callanan was always kind and reassuring to the young women, especially to new mothers. Between him and the good midwife they made sure the mother wasn't under too much pressure and was as comfortable as possible. Another stalwart from those times was the matron of the Cottage hospital, Matron Lane, who served the community well for over twenty years. She later became Matron Mc-Sweeney when she married Joe McSweeney. This good matron testified to Dr Callanan's conscientiousness in the care of his patients. His sense of humour was as good as a cure and we can only imagine the laughter in the wards as he had a joke or a cheery word for everybody. He visited the hospital daily and held dispensaries three days a week, morning and afternoon. As well as his care for the patients, he always showed concern for the staff, both nursing and domestic; he did not make distinctions. He was a straight-talking man, not known for mincing his words. There is a story told about a pious gentleman in the town who visited the dispensary complaining of diarrhoea. The good doctor suggested the tried and tested remedy known to all – a drop of brandy with a dash of port wine.

'Oh doctor, I couldn't possibly,' exclaimed the patient. 'What if anything happened, I could not meet my maker smelling of drink.'

'Well,' replied the doctor, 'it would be worse if you met him smelling of shit.'

He was a regular visitor to the KB as Philomena suffered from an illness which laid her low every three months, when she would be vomiting for days. She could hear him calling out to her as he reached the landing: 'You've got the gawkes again.' He would recommend a variety of cures hoping to stop the sickness but often it necessitated a trip to hospital and a few days on a drip. He referred her to various consultants who were as baffled as he was by this peculiar illness. She remembers him as being so very kind.

Phil well remembers his last visit to her father, the publican in the KB. They had known each since the days of the Troubles. He had to be helped up the stairs by Phil's brother as his hip was so painful and of course, like his patient, he was getting old, but the publican refused to see any other doctor. He sat on a chair and had a small drink and a good chat with the boss. It was sad to see these two great men bowed down by age and in the patient's case, ill health.

Fishing was another sport pursued by the doctor. He rented a house with his family in Courtmacsherry during the summer and spent a lot of time in his boat fishing. On one memorable occasion he was in the boat with his two friends: Joe Crowley, brother to Mary the famous midwife and Michael, a well known and well loved character in the town whose strange logic and wit was appreciated by all. On this particular day the boat sprang a leak. Joe and the doctor were busy pailing out the water while Michael sat up on top admiring the scenery. Joe called out to him to come down and help with the pailing out. 'I will not,' said Michael, 'I don't care if it sinks; it's not my boat at all.'

Coupled with his spirited good humour was a deep religious commitment which inspired Phil in her youth. Bandon's beloved doctor died in 1983 at the grand old age of eighty-five. His beloved Girlie outlived him by only six months. She died on their wedding anniversary, 1 January 1984. His memory will live on in Bandon for a long time to come because the stories will be told and his good deeds will be recounted from generation to generation.

12

The Christians' Tale

Bandon is a town of many religious denominations, all of whom have lived harmoniously together for many years. The Christian settlement allegedly made by St Brogan in the fifth century would suggest that Bandon has been Christian since the days of St Patrick. Little is known of St Brogan but Celtic scholars agree that he was a contemporary of St Patrick. The first settlers in the seventeenth century were puritans from the southwest of England, mainly Somerset and Devon, who shared names with many of those who sailed on the *Mayflower*. Queen Elizabeth I mandated that 'the citizens must be English and Protestant'; no Irish or Catholic person was permitted to live within the walls which were said to be taller, broader and stronger than the walls of Derry.

The story that the line 'Turk, Jew or Atheist may enter here but not a Papist' was written on the walls of Bandon has entered the annals of the town's history. According to the legend, some wit then wrote beneath it: 'The man who wrote it, wrote it well, for the same is written on the gates of hell.' These dictums owe more to folklore than to historical fact. Early in its history Bandon earned the name of being a town where even the pigs were Protestant!

Presbyterianism, a form of Protestant Christianity which developed after the Reformation, derives its name from the Greek word 'presbuteros' meaning 'elder'; the non-conformist churches were run by elders rather than by bishops. Presbyterian history can be traced back to John Calvin in Switzerland and to John Knox, a Scotsman who studied under Calvin and who persuaded the Scottish parliament to embrace the Reformation in 1560. In England, Presbyterianism was established in secret in 1572 towards the end of Elizabeth's reign. In Ireland, the Presbyterians, as well as the Catholics, suffered under the Penal Laws during the Long Parliament under the control of the puritans.

The Presbyterian congregation in Bandon is one of the oldest in the country. A large number of Scots, employed by the earls of Bandon, swelled the numbers of this already popular church. The Reverend John Hazlitt, father of the famous essayist William Hazlitt, ministered here from 1780 to 1783. He was honoured for his defence of the rights of the citizens of the town and of the American prisoners in Kinsale jail. The Presbyterians used a church on Kilbrogan Hill which dated back to 1628, a mere twenty-four years after the founding of the town. The manse and schoolhouse in Bandon were built by the dynamic minister, Mr Irwin, who served in Bandon from 1855 to 1875. He was succeeded by the Reverend Thomas Brown who, with his wife, Sarah, served the Bandon Presbyterian congregation for nearly fifty years until he was joined by his son, Thomas Rentual Brown, in 1932.

Thomas was born in 1895, the youngest of six children. He attended the Presbyterian school in Watergate Street and received his secondary education at the manse from his governess, Miss Neilson. All courses at the manse school were of full matriculation standard. It became known as one of the more reputable schools and many of the prominent families in town sent their children there. In later years his sister, Elfie, ran the school. His other sisters were Margaret, Irene and Zoe; his older brother, James, who was a student for the ministry, died in 1914 aged twenty-three.

After matriculation young Thomas went to Trinity College, Dublin, from where he graduated in 1917. He went on to study theology at the Presbyterian college in Belfast. He served in Lisburn and at Clifden Street, Belfast, before returning to assist his father in Bandon and Clonakilty, eventually becoming his successor. In 1937, he married Phyllis Geraldine Jones of the Green, Bandon. They had three children: Ann, Gervais and Daphne, who still lives in Bandon and is married to Bob Deane, a business man in town.

Mr Brown had a huge parish to cover throughout all of west and north Cork stretching from Oysterhaven to Millstreet, taking in Bantry and Castletownbere. Mr Brown never had the luxury of an automobile and had to travel many, many miles by bus, train and boat to visit his flock. He was an athletic man and a great swimmer, having swum the English Channel as a young man. He continued to swim well into his eighties.

By 1959, his congregation had dwindled to as few as sixty-three people and from 1970, services were held at the manse. Mrs Brown died in 1977 and the minister died of a heart attack in December 1979. He had served his flock well, being renowned for his pastoral care. Nearly four hundred years of history died with him as he was the last Presbyterian minister in Bandon.

Tales abound of the minister's generosity and integrity. He never failed to visit a bereaved family in the area. Both he and his wife had a smile and kind word for everybody. The most famous story of the minister's integrity is the tale of the rents of the absentee landlord, Mr Munt. Mr Brown stopped collecting the rent, suspecting that Mr Munt had died. This of course meant that the tenants could keep their houses under the squatters' rights law.

Tommy Canniffe's grandmother worked at the manse, cooking and cleaning for the Brown family whom she loved. She was always loud in her praise of them. The minister kept a cow and Tommy benefited from his generosity on one occasion when the cow was about to calf. The minister ran across the road and asked the young Tommy to summon Mr Donovan who lived in the last house in Foxes Street and who also worked at the manse, to come and help deliver the calf. Tommy obliged and the next day the minister came to the house and gave him two shillings – a lot of money back then.

෨

Methodism grew among the settlers in Bandon in much the same way as it grew in Wales and England. People became disillusioned with the established church, with its pomp and splendour so the idea of personal conversion and the simplicity of the service appealed to the ordinary people. John Wesley, – who with his brother Charles founded Methodism – visited Bandon in 1748, a mere twenty years after the foundation of the sect. In all John Wesley visited Bandon seventeen times between 1748 and 1789. His brother Charles only visited Bandon once and is said to have composed one of his famous hymns en route. William Murray, who was a resident of Cork in 1748, moved to Bandon in the same year and became the leading supporter of Methodism in the town. The early missionaries stayed in his home and his son John wrote in his autobiography that he had been appointed a class leader over a class of forty young Methodist boys by John Wesley. John Murray went on to become a Methodist Preacher in America where he died in 1815.

A chapel was built on Kilbrogan Hill in 1760, on the site where the old vocational school was later built. However Methodism grew quickly in Bandon and overcrowding soon became a problem in the chapel. A new building was erected in North Main Street which later became the boys' club, but is now demolished. In his eighty-sixth year John Wesley paid his last visit to Bandon to open this chapel. He had visited the town about nineteen times in all; such was the importance he placed on the growing congregation in Bandon. When the congregation outgrew this building, the duke of Devonshire donated the present site on Bandon Bridge plus a sum of £250 to the Methodists. The church is still used for worship and has a congregation of about seventy people.

***

The Christian Brethren or Plymouth Brethren met at the Riverside Hall in Watergate Street. Their remit was to restore Christianity to its original simplicity. Their first recorded meeting took place in 1840. That congregation has joined the Baptist Union of Ireland and has, according to Billy Smith of Spring Lane, an active congregation of about seventy souls. Known as 'Westside Baptist Chapel', they meet for worship in their new chapel built during the 1980's in the village of Old Chapel.

***

The first Quaker community in Bandon was formed by Francis Howgill in 1655. George Fox, the founder of the Quakers, visited Bandon some years later and gave his name to 'Foxes Street'. The Quakers had their meeting house in Weir Street and were active in Bandon for over 150 years. They were a gentle people who 'walked their talk' and who looked after the starving Irish during the famine. Their contribution to famine sufferers has often been discredited because of tales of 'soup for conversion' – a form of proselytising – but these stories have no basis in fact. They provided soup kitchens for the starving and there is no evidence of any hidden agendas. The Quakers have always been at the forefront of highlighting social justice and humanitarian issues.

လာ

The Unitarian church was built in 1813 and was attended mainly by the Allman and Dowden families and their workers. With the demise of the milling and distilling industries and the mass emigration that followed it, the church fizzled out.

လာ

In 1849, St Peter's Church was consecrated by the Bishop of Killaloe, Co. Clare, a relative of the Bernard family. It replaced Christ Church as the main place of worship for the Church of Ireland congregation; an earlier church, built in 1614, had existed on this site. Christ Church in North Main Street was the first church built in Ireland for Protestant worship. All the others had been confiscated from the Catholics after the Reformation. The two sites at Kilbrogan and Ballymodan had churches dating back to the thirteenth century, long before the Reformation. Parish priests of Bandon, many of whom are buried in Kilbrogan cemetery, can be traced back to that date.

လာ

In 1796, the Countess of Bandon gave land in Gallows Hill for the building of a Catholic church, in gratitude for her son's recovery from a serious illness. Her husband, the earl, donated money for the building and paid the rent for the site. Many of the business people of the town also contributed to the project. The Catholics of Bandon had worshipped in a church in Old Chapel, which is now Crowley's Yard, until the Gallows Hill Church opened in 1779. Fr Shinnick, parish priest of Bandon from 1779 to 1814, was the first priest to serve in this church. The now redundant St Fintan's school stands on the site.

In 1856, William Delaney laid the foundation stone for a magnificent new church, St Patrick's. He was alleged to have been born in the sacristy of Kilbrogan Church during the Christmas mass of 1804 and he went on to become bishop of Cork from 1845 to 1847. The parish priest responsible for the building of St Patrick's was Fr Jeremiah O'Brien who served the Bandon community until 1878.

There are numerous stories about the many incumbents of the Bandon Catholic parish. The venues for the 'station masses' were read out every Sunday to the great amusement of the children who could name every parish in the area. The mass was said in the stipulated house and all the neighbours came. At the station mass each household paid their 'dues' to the clergy. The system in town was different: the priests visited every house in town to collect the dues. On one occasion a priest who was a keen golfer called to one of his parishioners and asked the lady of the house why her children were not at school.

'Because they have no shoes, Father,' was her reply.

'Well, that is no cause for shame,' said the priest. 'Sure, Jesus had no shoes.'

'No,' replied the quick-witted lady, 'and he had no golf clubs either.'

The first Corpus Christi procession was held in Bandon in 1933. It was introduced by Fr Martin Murphy, who succeeded Fr Jeremiah Cohalan as parish priest; Jeremiah was Bishop Daniel Cohalan's brother. It was the year which followed the Eucharistic Congress in Dublin so devotion to the Blessed Sacrament was becoming popular. In those days the Bandon Corpus Christi processions were something to behold: the town was adorned with an abundance of flowers, bunting, statues and altars.

Every house had an altar in the window and flags flying. It was an extraordinary expression of faith and devotion. Every Catholic man, woman and child – anybody who could walk – took part. The first communion and confirmation children looked resplendent in their outfits, the girls wearing white dresses and veils and the boys in their smart shirts, ties and trousers, wearing sashes. The Children of Mary formed a sea of blue in their lovely cloaks. There was a men's section and a women's section – many of the women dressed in the traditional hooded cloak. Each section was led by a member of the Legion of Mary carrying a banner. The school children walked together wearing their uniforms. The procession was one of the most important days in the town's calendar and everybody was busy in the weeks leading up to it, cleaning, washing and painting their properties so that all was pristine on the great day.

It was early in the nineteenth century before the first Catholic set up business in the town; Paddy Gaffney was given permission to open a shop in the main street. This was the first sight of a Catholic for many of the inhabitants and they were rather curious about him. On discovering that he was no different from themselves, they got on well with him and of course he 'opened the door' and soon there were many Catholic businesses in the town. When the 1834 census was taken it showed an equal number of Protestant and Catholic residents.

13

THE CAR-MAKER'S TALE

'I came among you and you took me in.' This was the opening sentence of Henry Ford's speech on a visit to his father's native county, when the locals cheated him by adding an extra zero to the already hefty cheque he had donated to the community from whence his father emigrated during the famine.

Henry's father was twenty-one in 1847 when the entire family left the small village of Ballinascarthy, between Bandon and Clonakilty. The Ford party of emigrants comprised the seventy-six-year-old widow, Rebecca Ford; her son, John and his wife, Thomasina, from Fair Lane, Cork City, accompanied by their seven children, of whom William was the eldest; and another of Rebecca's sons, Robert, with his wife and family of four. Sadly, Thomasina Ford did not survive the journey to the New World.

On arrival in Canada the family headed for Dearborn, near

Quebec, where three of Rebecca's sons had already settled when they emigrated in 1832. They were now all farming in the area. John bought a farm and with his mother and young family, settled down to work.

William did not enjoy farming so he went to work for the Michigan Railway Company. Eventually he returned to work for a farmer named Ahern who also hailed from Cork. Some years later he married the Aherns' adopted daughter, Mary Litogot. After the marriage, the young William and Mary moved into another farm near Dearborn where they were surrounded by their relatives. They had six children, of whom Henry, born on 30 July 1863, was the eldest.

Henry, like his father, did not like farming, so he moved around Michigan doing a variety of jobs. He worked as a machinist's assistant and a watchmaker but he soon moved on to repairing and maintaining steam engines. He had a shed on the farm where he tinkered with engines and by the age of fifteen he had constructed his first steam engine. He also worked for a time as an engineer for the Edison Electrical Company which supplied electric light to the city of Detroit.

When he was about thirty Henry became involved with the internal combustion engine and in 1896, when he was thirty-three years old, he built his first car, the Quadricycle. This crude-looking vehicle had four big bicycle wheels and was steered with a tiller, like a boat. It had only two forward speeds and no reverse. From this humble beginning grew the motor giant we know today. Ford was the first mass producer of motorcars, revolutionising the automobile industry and doubling the wages of manual workers. He was just forty years old when the first Ford motorcar was sold.

Henry never forgot his roots. In 1912, he travelled back to Cork to visit the farm at Ballinascarthy and the cottage at Fair Lane in Cork. Such was his love for Cork and for his ancestors that he named his mansion in Detroit 'Fair Lane' in memory of the place his great-grandmother, his grandparents and his father spent their last night in Ireland before escaping from a life of poverty and hardship. The housing estate which he built for his workforce was also called 'Fair Lane' and the Ford Fair Lane was one of his most successful cars.

The Ford Motor Company's Cork plant was established at the Marina in 1917. It was here that the first Ford tractors, outside America, were made. The company was welcomed by one and all. George Crosbie, owner of the *Cork Examiner*, wrote: 'The project marked the true industrial development of Cork city and port and indeed the whole of Ireland generally.' Daniel Cohalan, bishop of Cork, said simply, 'Welcome Home Henry.' Lord Mayor Tomás MacCurtain visited the plant and gave it his seal of approval. The plant gave employment to thousands of men from the Cork area and improved the quality of life of as many families. They were paid a fair wage and for the first time people had money in their pockets.

In 1929, the Ford Motor Company opened in Dagenham in Essex where the tractor manufacturing operation was now located and Cork became a car-assembly plant only.

During the war years many Cork people moved to England for war service, where workers were in short supply. Because great numbers of the Cork workforce were experienced in tractor production, they headed for Dagenham, a town which became known as 'little Cork'. Huge housing estates were built to accommodate these workers and their families.

In 1950, Pat Wilmot left Boyle Street in Bandon having been recruited by the British ministry of labour to work in Ford's. There was no work for him at home so he had to 'take the boat' like many of his friends had done. Pat, the only person from Bandon, accompanied by many young men from Cork, took the train to Dublin and headed for the Globe Hotel, a place remembered with contempt by many an Irish emigrant. He spent two nights there, underwent a medical examination and was subjected to the most degrading assault on his person – being deloused with DDT. This practice was considered 'necessary' because the young men who came from turf growing areas might be infested with lice. Pat, who came from a spotlessly clean home and whose person and clothing were immaculate, was too shy to protest.

By the third day the young men, about thirty-five in all, were glad to get on the boat to Holyhead to begin their new lives. At the port they boarded the steam train and headed for Euston Station, London, where they were met by Ford personnel who travelled with them by bus to Dagenham. Here they underwent another medical; clearly the Ford Motor Company did not have any confidence in the Globe's medical officers. Tired and weary from the journey and missing his home and family, Pat remembers the hostel they stayed in at Chadwell Heath. It had formerly been a prisoner-of-war camp and now afforded comfortable but temporary accommodation until the company housed them with one of their approved landladies. On that first morning Pat travelled from this hostel on the No. 175 bus which stopped outside the Ford motor plant. He asked the conductress if the bus was going to Ford's to which she retorted, 'Well darling, I'll be very disappointed if it doesn't.' It was all so strange – the accents, the buses, the buildings and oh, so many people – a far cry from Boyle Street where everybody knew and understood everybody else.

Ford's had a welfare and personnel officer who made sure that every young Irish lad got decent lodgings. Digs were found for Pat with a kind lady in Barking – a lady he remembers with great affection. He stayed there for two years until her illness caused him to leave. None of his subsequent lodgings were as pleasant as this, his first 'home from home'. He recalls being thrown out of other digs by the landlady because he had the audacity to switch on the light on a dark Sunday afternoon when he was playing cards with the landlord.

That first morning when Pat reported for work he was amazed at the scale of the place. The whole works was nearly as large as Bandon and he wondered if he would ever find his way around. He worked two shifts, one week of nights and one week of days, a gruelling system which continued for eight years, until the more manageable three-shift pattern was introduced: early, late and nights. He continued with this system until 1985, when the foundry closed.

Sir Patrick Hennessy another Irish man, was managing director of Ford's during Pat's time there and he was a kind and fair boss. When Pat started work in 1950 there were 38,000 people employed there, most of whom were from Cork city and county. The pay and conditions were good and people were happy with their lot. All Ford employees agree that it was a good company to work for. The plant closed down for the last two weeks in August every year when the workers came home and enjoyed themselves in their native place. In the early days they came up the river in the Innisfallen to the city centre, singing as they arrived and still singing two weeks later as they departed. With the building of Cork Airport flying became more convenient for them, eliminating the long journey to south Wales followed by the boat journey from Swansea or Fishguard.

Pat could not come home so regularly at first until he managed to save some money. In 1955, he got engaged to his childhood sweetheart, Nora, who followed him to Essex in 1957. She had managed to get good digs in Romford – in those days cohabiting was unheard of! She worked in a local grocery store, an employment with which she was familiar having worked in J.P. Deasy's grocery store in Bandon since leaving school. She married her beloved Pat on 28 March 1958. They had to have a special dispensation for the wedding which took place during Lent, but they needed the tax rebate as a down payment on their house. They bought a house in Hornchurch, where their three children, Elizabeth, Annette and Gerard were born and where they lived until they returned to Bandon in 1997. When the children were older Nora went back to work, getting a job at St Ursula's School. In 1978, she moved to the London Stock Exchange where she remained until her retirement in 1994.

Their faith was very important to Pat and Nora – like many young people leaving Ireland the advice was to 'keep the faith and never eat black pudding on a Friday'. Many of the emigrants, true to their faith, were responsible for the building of Catholic churches throughout England. As well as supporting family at home, they supported the spread of Catholicism in England. When Pat and Nora married there was no Catholic church in either Romford or Hornchurch; they had to walk a half an hour to mass each Sunday and on holy days. Between shift work and small children this needed heroic effort, but they managed it. Nora, a beautiful singer, who had been a member of the church choir before she left Bandon, continued to sing in church in her adopted home.

In 1961, permission was granted for the building of a church in Hornchurch. While the money for this was being raised, mass was celebrated in the local pub and later in a prefabricated building. By the middle 1970s the church had become a reality and the prefabricated building became the church hall. Pat and Nora's contribution to the enhancement of their host country has been enormous and all the time they continued to send the few bob back to their families at home. They also took care of other emigrants – many young Irish people leaving home for the first time had their paths smoothed by the work of these pioneers. Even Phil benefited from the wisdom and generosity of these humble people from her home town, when she emigrated to Wales in 1975.

The Mill House was a club built by the local council at Dagenham and even though the Ford Motor Company had provided three clubs for the relaxation of its workforce, most of the Cork people seemed to favour the Mill House, making up ninety-five per cent of the patrons. Phil visited the club in 1976 and as she listened to the Cork accents, the sing song and the craic, she almost fancied she was back in the Kilmichael Bar. Sadly, with the reduction of the workforce, the Mill House is home to only the few remaining old men who were the founding fathers of so many facilities for the Irish in southeast England. Pat and Nora are enjoying a well earned retirement in their native Bandon. Pat cares for his garden and has the odd pint in the Kilmichael Bar with his friend, Thomas Crean. Nora still sings in the church choir and can be persuaded on special occasions – during Phil's visits – to sing the odd song in the KB, reminiscent of the many happy sessions they enjoyed together in the old days.

14

THE BANDLEADER'S TALE

Bandon can boast of more dance bands than any other town of its size in Ireland. In the 1920s one such band was the Allin Institute Band which met, practised and played there when it was in its heyday. John Mel Poland – a beautiful concert class pianist – set up this accordion band in the 1930s. The following song, to the air of 'The Rising of the Moon', was written about its members when they were at the height of their popularity around 1937. The highlight of the year was their New Year's Eve jaunt around the town in a 'wagonette' driven by Jake Sweeney:

As I was out last New Year's Eve
I thought I heard a band,
And through the streets of Bandon
The music sounded grand.

When Geraldín played up
Auld Lang Syne
The tune for old time's sake
The horse stopped dead and shook his head
And 'twas harmonised by Jake.
They played around the town
That night,
'Twas worth your while to wait.
They played us out of '37 and into '38.

(Author unknown, but probably written by Lizzy May Cohalan)

The band played at a variety of stops around the town, including Foxes Street Cross where the clientele of the Kilmichael Bar joined in the general music, dance and merriment. The members of the band were John Mel, Gerald Jones, Jimmy Roche, Jackie Coughlan and Frankie Lyons. Unfortunately, the band was broken up by the Spanish Civil War when John Mel and Jimmy Roche, along with several young men from the town, went off to fight for Franco. Some of the members got together again later as the Romany Band and entertained Bandonians until the band's demise in the mid 1940s.

The Cohalan Brothers' Band was formed in 1953 by Mickey and Anthony – Lizzy May's sons. It consisted of Michael Crean, known locally as Ginger, whose wonderful singing voice earned him the name 'The Golden Voiced Crooner', Richard Dukelow and Gerard Beirne, a Co. Roscommon man who had come to teach science at the Hamilton High School.

Tadhg McCarthy and Tom Kenny – who had been a trumpeter in a British army band – joined up later. If the hall happened to have a piano, Lizzy May would also accompany the band as a pianist. When the Clavioline organ came on the market, the Cohalan Brothers' Band was the first band in Ireland to purchase one. All the band members had day jobs so their playing consisted of weekend bookings or perhaps a night or two during the week. They played throughout the counties of Cork and Kerry and once did two weeks at the 'Summer Season' at Crosshaven, a popular holiday resort in the 1950s and 1960s.

Before forming his own band, Mickey had played with John Larkin. The Larkin brothers, John and Michael, had been making music in town for many years and when Mickey left two bands were formed: the Cohalan Brothers and the Ritz Showband. Anthony Cohalan recalls, 'Many's the time we would be seen leaving Bandon at four o'clock in the afternoon in an old Comer van weighed down with a double bass laced to the roof, not to return again until about seven o'clock the following morning and all for £2 a man.' Sadly, this band broke up in 1958. Anthony joined the Olympic Showband in Dunmanway and later the Bohemians which was based in Barryroe.

Mickey Cohalan was regarded as the Mick Delahunty of Bandon. He was a man with an outstanding musical talent and when it came to electrics he was a genius. Born in June 1925 he was Lizzy May's eldest son. He was a serious-minded young boy who enjoyed gymnastics and singing. He was blessed with a beautiful voice and sang in the church choir along with many other young boys from the town. As a small boy he was part of Canon Murphy's Angel Choir which sang from the church tower on Christmas Eve 1932. When Mickey was about thirteen years old he won a singing competition which was broadcast on Radio Éireann. Frank Donovan – who played Battie Brennan in 'The Riordans' back in the late 1960s and composed that well-known Bandon song 'Sitting on the Bridge below the Town' – was conducting a talent search for Radio Éireann around the towns of Ireland. Mickey sang 'Santa Lucia' and won the boys' section; Chrissie Buston from Castle Road won the girls' section.

Mickey frequently played for his mother's classes and also at the *feiseanna* when the dancers from the Cohalan School of Dancing were competing. While other boys of his age were out playing, Mickey would be tinkering with a wireless or trying to discover the components of some other piece of electrical equipment. He loved music; he could play any instrument but he mainly played the piano accordion and the flute.

He studied electronics at the vocational school and then served his time with Robin Begley, who was part of a big electrical business in Bandon during the 1950s and 1960s. When he had completed his apprenticeship he went to Mallow and worked as an electrician in the sugar beet factory. Later he moved to Portarlington where he spent some time working for the ESB. These jobs were short-lived however because

Mickey missed his beloved Bandon and his musical family. Nevertheless he was not idle; he studied every evening until he gained further qualifications in electronics, by correspondence course, obtaining his A.M.I.E.T., Associate Member of the Institute of Engineering Technology. He went to London hoping to gain some more experience and worked for Cosser, a company at the forefront of radio and television production. While in England, he studied and acquired his M.R.S.G.B. certificate, Member of the Radio Society of Great Britain. He could take a radio or television apart and put it back together again before anybody in Ireland even possessed a television.

With these qualifications to his credit he returned to Bandon in 1950 and opened his own business in the New Road. His younger brother, Anthony, became his first apprentice. Soon he had four apprentices. His sisters, Mercy and Celia, helped with the book-keeping and supervised the shop while Mickey was out with his apprentices maintaining the electrical systems at Beamish's brewery, Brennan's mill, the West Cork Bottling Company, Hartes, or one of the other major businesses in Bandon or the surrounding area. He had all the main local electrical contracts.

During all this time Mickey was a teetotaller; he still had his confirmation pledge when he was twenty-nine years old. In the Ireland of those days, children became pioneers when they made their confirmation at the age of twelve or thirteen, with the hope that they would re-commit to the Pioneer Total Abstinence Association when they reached the age of twenty-one. In his thirtieth year, Mickey developed a nasty chest infection which did not seem to be clearing up. He was working hard at the time doing his electrical work by day and playing in the band at night and didn't think much of it. His doctor sent him to be checked by the mobile tuberculosis testing unit which came regularly to the town where they discovered he had a shadow on his lung. He was advised to take a glass of stout every day because of its high iron content. This was a regular tonic or 'pick me up' in those days – a glass of warm stout for adults or stout with milk and sugar for children. Being a conscientious young man Mickey did as he was advised but disaster followed.

An excellent business man, Mickey started the practice of joining other business men of the town for a few drinks at the Munster Arms Hotel. There each patron had his own seat and God help anybody who unknowingly occupied the seat of one of the regulars; the culprits would be ordered to move by the intrepid barmaid, Mary Meagher. Mickey had started on the slippery slope and so began his journey down the lonely road of the alcoholic. His behaviour changed; he didn't seem to care about anything but the next drink. Soon his drinking was out of control; he became a 'happy' drunk, singing and playing music. Al Jolson songs became the order of the day, especially 'The Spaniard that Blighted my Life', which was his favourite. This soon became his way of life: the life and soul of the party, a party which continued night and day, in any pub, with any company. His musical talent, which was his greatest gift, now became his biggest problem, since he was plied with drinks in lieu of payment, as he entertained on the piano or piano accordion the patrons of many pubs, including the Kilmichael Bar. He attracted many 'friends' prepared to help divest him of his money and indulge his self pity. His family were in despair and their pain must have been excruciating. Their talented brother who was always so sensible and reliable now seemed a stranger to them. This was the man who had built his own electric organ before such instruments were heard of in Ireland by taking the keys from an old piano and collecting the other bits and pieces necessary to complete the project. Now he could only think about alcohol and his disease was progressing rapidly.

Soon Mickey lost his business, in spite of Anthony's best efforts to keep it going – a difficult task with his brother drawing off it all the time. Mickey became more and more alcohol dependent. People tried to avoid him and the 'friends' disappeared when the money ran out.

It was at this time that Phil got to know Mickey. She was immediately attracted by his vulnerability, his sensitive nature and his childlike quality of love and trust regardless of his drunken state. He was quietly spoken and his jokes were always clean. Phil never heard him swear. Somehow, she saw through the damage being done to the soul of this lovely man and she began to think of ways of helping him. However she was naïve and knew as little as everybody else about the disease that was killing him.

His health began to fail and he had to be hospitalised, doing the rounds of several hospitals. He was well cared for and much loved by the staff and other patients who saw him for the nice, sensitive, courteous man that he was. With improved health he would be released from hospital and head straight for the nearest pub. Then the whole sorry cycle started all over again – hospital, pub, back to hospital, until he eventually contracted TB and was confined to the sanatorium for several months.

While there he was introduced to the twelve steps of Alcoholics Anonymous and the miracle happened: he committed to them. By the time he left the sanatorium, he was fragile and much depleted in health, but sober. He went to live with his sister, Mercy and brother-in-law, Tommy and their family in Ballineen. They supported and helped him in every way, making sure he attended his weekly AA meetings. Surrounded by love, he made his daily commitment to AA and continued to live his life by the twelve steps. He went regularly to Myross Wood near Leap – a retreat house run by the Sacred Heart Fathers – where he found the peace and tranquillity he needed for his recovery.

Very slowly he began to piece his life together again. He started to play music with his nieces and nephews, all of whom had inherited the family gift of music and dance. Those who loved him were justly proud of his final and strenuous battle against the force of alcoholism. His body cried out for the drug but his spiritual resources were such that he was able to say no. Only a recovering addict could appreciate the magnitude of Mickey's struggle. He was also a regular visitor to the Rosminian House at Upton, which had been an Industrial School and is now a home for young adult males with special needs still run by the Rosminians. He recognised that Christmas was a difficult time for alcoholics and so normally spent the festive season entertaining the boys who were resident there. On his last Christmas it snowed and as he played the piano and led the sing-song, he saw Father Christmas coming up the avenue with his bag of gifts for the residents – he said it was truly magical. He confided to his sister, Celia, when he visited her on St Stephen's Day, that it was 'the happiest, holiest, most peaceful and enjoyable Christmas of my whole life'. Two months later he was dead.

He was fifty-nine years old when he died. Comments were made at the time of the talent he had wasted through alcoholism but many, including Phil, strongly disagreed with such remarks. She believes that he struggled from the depths of his being to regain his dignity and he won. She is proud to have been numbered among his special friends. It was with much pride that she learned of his visit to the Convent of Mercy secondary school in Kinsale in the late 1970s as part of a group invited to talk to the students about alcoholism. All present were moved by his story and by his integrity.

15

THE TALE OF THE SPEECH AND DRAMA TEACHER

The reason Bandon women of a certain age articulate so beautifully is because at some time during their trajectory through primary school they were taught by Sr Alphonsus O'Brien. This Maria von Trapp of the Presentation Convent Bandon must have been a breath of fresh air when she arrived there in the 1940s as a bubbly teenager. She admits to running up the stairs, two steps at the time, singing at the top of her voice. She was not only an asset to the convent, but to her adopted town, county and yes, to the whole of Ireland.

Sr Alphonsus, who hails from Limerick, comes from a musical family. Her grandfather received a silver baton at Crystal Palace London as bandleader of the Boherbury Band – a brass and reed band. Her father, also a talented musician, who wrote the music for his band by hand, won prizes with a *céilí* band of students from the vocational school where he taught. Her mother was a lovely singer. The young Alphonsus received a good education at an interdenominational school in Limerick, the Model School. From this school she went on to the Presentation Convent, near Thurles, where she boarded. It was during her time there that she developed her dramatic skills, taking leading roles in the school plays. She sat her elocution diploma while a student, becoming a fellow of the London College of Music. She also travelled to Dublin for mime lessons with Professor Dodding of the BBC.

As a young student, Alphonsus was inspired by the stories of Nano Nagle – that indomitable lady from near Mallow who founded the Presentation Order during Penal times. Nano had the benefit of an education in Paris but returned to Ireland when her father died in 1746. She and her mother set up house in Dublin, where she witnessed the most horrific effects of the Penal laws on her people. The most wretched were the children. She wondered how she could help them and decided that prayer was her only option, so she entered a convent in France. Like St Patrick, the memories of the poor children on the streets of Dublin haunted her. After much prayer and soul-searching, she sought advice from her spiritual director, who confirmed her conviction that her calling was to instruct the Irish children.

Nano came to Cork and opened her first school – a mud cabin – which housed thirty children. Less than a year later there were two hundred children – all girls – in two or more cabins. Added to her teaching, she visited the old, the sick and the poor of Cork in their homes. However she felt the need for some kind of organisation to stabilise the work she was doing. Under the guidance of the French Jesuits, she decided to introduce a religious community. The French Ursalines agreed to train four Irish girls for the Cork foundation. Unfortunately for Nano the Ursalines were an enclosed order so they could not go out to the schools; furthermore, they were founded for the education of the rich whereas Nano's mission was to educate the poor catholic children of Ireland. Not daunted by this setback she invited a group of young Cork women to join her in her work in 1775. From this fledgling group that great order of educators – the Presentation Sisters – was founded. Nano is regarded as the pioneer of Catholic education in the modern world. What idealistic young woman could fail to be inspired by Nano Nagle's story?

Alphonsus knew she wanted to be part of this adventure. She looked at a number of Presentation Convents before settling for Bandon. The Presentation Convent in Bandon had been founded in 1829 by a Skibbereen woman named Catherine O'Neill, who came with her mother to make the foundation. Lady Bandon gifted the sisters five acres of land outside the town walls where they built their convent and school. Almost two hundred years later the convent remains: a monument to the selfless dedication of these women to the education of young people.

Sr Alphonsus could have graced any world stage with her talent and ability but she chose instead to devote her time and her boundless energy to the promotion of the careers of others. Her family's grief can only be imagined as they watched the moving ceremony of her reception into the Presentation Order. Dressed as a bride she wore a beautiful white dress and a veil of exquisite Limerick lace, which had been made by the sisters of the Bandon community. Two years later, in the absence of the Bishop, she made her temporary vows to his delegate, Fr Fulham – whose family had a pub in Shannon Street – had the honour. After a further three years she made her final profession in the presence of Bishop Cornelius Lucey and committed to the Presentation charism for life. That was over fifty years ago.

Her first teaching assignment was with the infants and she says she was never happier than when she was with them. She was an inspired teacher with a natural talent for the job. By the time Phil and her friend Noreen Spillane (Lehane) caught up with her, she was teaching fourth class and she actually progressed with them on to fifth and sixth classes. They were already well acquainted with Alphonsus from their Saturday elocution classes, which they had been attending since they started school. In those days there were elocution examinations, *feiseanna* and the highlight of the year, *Cór Fhéile na Scol*, a singing and drama competition for schools. Phil and her classmates of the late 1950s have graced the stage of Cork City Hall as dwarves, chickens, choir members and dancers, in all manner of costumes made by the parents.

Since those days Sr Alphonsus and her various troupes have won many competitions and cups, including winning the famous Sinead de Valera trophy for *Féilé Ceol Dramaíochta na Scol* (the School's Musical Drama Festival) eight times. The plays were Alphonsus' own plots and ideas which were translated into Irish by Fr Horgan, a distinguished Irish scholar. The Bandon Dramatic Society which she founded in the early 1970s has won drama competitions at the Rossmore Drama Festival several times. They staged such challenging plays as *The Playboy of the Western World* and *An Inspector Calls*. She is still teaching elocution in a variety of schools and to young seminarians. Her name is a by-word in speech and drama circles the length and breadth of Ireland and no doubt the many emigrants whom she taught still reminisce about their 'stage days'. She has even been entertained by the former president, Mary Robinson, although the question is: who was entertaining whom! Sr Alphonsus has certainly lived the Presentation charism to the full, both as a semi-enclosed sister and as a sister active in her local community, in true Nano Nagle style.

16

THE SOLDIERS' TALE

The Walsh family lived at 13 Boyle Street; the family consisted of six children, two girls and four boys. Mary Brigid emigrated to America and Mary Jane married Cornelius Linehan. Three of the boys joined the forces. Tommy, after service in the First World War, went to America and rose to the rank of commanding officer in the American navy. John and Connie joined the British army. Tommy was a playing member of the Bandon Workingman's Fife and Drum Band while John and Connie were ordinary members. All have been highly praised for their courage and have been given a place of honour in the recording of the First World War. Michael, who was too young to join the army, was the only boy who remained in Bandon. He later married and lived opposite the KB. He had three daughters and one son: Bridie, who has recently retired to Bandon; Sheila, who lives in England; Bernadette, who emigrated to Australia; and Paddy, who lives in England.

The young John Walsh was an elegant gentleman, always beautifully dressed with waistcoat and fob watch in place. His wife, Ann, who came from Innishannon, travelled with him as an army cook. He saw action in North Africa and the Far East where he rose to the rank of sergeant. After the war he worked in England as a butler, with Ann as a cook in the big houses. His party piece – and he had a fine voice – was 'The Road to Mandelay'. It sounded so exotic to the children of the KB. His brother, Connie, did not marry and so lived with his mother after his discharge from the army. He was a painter and decorator. The two brothers were very close friends and always came together in the early evening, sitting in the tap room of the KB at either side of the fire, savouring their few pints.

Men who experienced the horrors of war spoke little about it and John was often irritated by the pub talk of two gentlemen who had never seen any action at home or abroad. On a particular evening one of these gentlemen was relating how he had stood black and tans up against the wall while the other gentleman shot them. Irritated by this fantasy, John put him straight one night with the words, 'For goodness sake, man, my wife did more soldiering than you ever saw.'

When he was in the Dardanelles he wrote the following letter to his mother in Boyle Street:

H.Q. A Coy 1st Royal Munster Fusiliers

86th Brigade

29th Division – B.E.F.

Dardanelles

Turkey

Dear Mother,

I received your last letter the last week of April. I am delighted to hear all the family are quite well. We are in the best of health ourselves that is what is left of us. We had several engagements with the Turks. I am quite safe so far, not wounded yet, thank God. Jimmie Searles got killed in the first engagement. Connie is quite safe also Dan Whelton. It is pretty warm here by day and very cold by night. I had a letter on the 9th from Mrs Sewell, she is quite well, she told me she writes to you regularly. I wish this thing was over, so would all the boys. I hope it will be all over soon. There is nothing much to tell. We are not allowed to say much. When it is all over we can spin a few yarns.

Our regiment and the Royal Dublin Fusiliers made a name for themselves. If what we done gets in the papers the people will have something to read about and will be proud of the two Irish regiments.

Dear mother will you send me out a few papers every week, that's all we want, we get plenty to eat and enough tobacco to carry on with, the only thing we get too much of is the enemy shrapnel and bullets. Give my love to Dad,

Babe and Bid. Did you get any account of Tommy yet? I hope he will get back all right, he is much better off in France than we are here. No more to say this time. Good-bye for a while. With love to all. Remember me to Mrs Sewell.

I remain your loving son

John.

(Letter printed by kind permission of Billy Good and the
Bandon War Memorial Committee)

The Jimmy Searles he spoke of was one of Annie and Thomas Searles' sons. In all, they had nine children: six sons and three daughters. Most of the family later emigrated. Three of the boys, Henry, Edward and James (Jimmy), joined the British army at the outbreak of the First World War. All three were awarded medals for bravery and distinction. James had been a member of the famous Bandon Working Men's Fife and Drum Band.

There are many reasons why young men go to war but most of them have little to do with ideology. Usually, it is those with least to defend who are on the front line and it was the same in this case; the sons of poor Irish families who had no jobs and no prospects hoped to make a career for themselves in the forces. Some joined for adventure. Tom Barry, who has carved a place in Irish history as the leader of guerrilla warfare in West Cork with his flying column, joined 'to see what war was like, to get a gun, to see new countries and to feel like a grown man'. No doubt these were the sentiments of many as they headed for the front. Our own W.B Yeats summed up the Irish position fairly well in his famous poem, 'An Irish Airman Foresees his Death' in the lines:

> Those that I fight I do not hate,
> Those that I guard I do not love.

John Redmond of the Nationalist Party committed the nationalists to the war in the hope that home rule would be achieved as a result. The Catholic church recommended that Ireland should go to the defence of little Catholic Belgium – the 'Defence of Small Nations' propaganda. The propaganda machine told the young men that they would be home for Christmas.

210,000 Irish men and women served in the British forces. Remembering that there was no conscription this is a staggering number. Another 140,000 joined during the war as volunteers. In all, 35,000 Irishmen died in this conflict – our forgotten heroes.

Francis Ledwidge, poet, nationalist and Trade Unionist, is said to have gone to war on the rebound from an unhappy love affair. He had a chequered career, being apprenticed to a grocer at the age of fifteen, going on to become a farm worker, a groom, a road worker and a copper miner and writing poetry all the while. He is listed among the anti-war poets but is best remembered in Ireland for his poem about Thomas McDonagh – one of the executed 1916 heroes:

He shall not hear the bittern cry
In the wild sky where he is lain,
Nor the voices of the sweeter birds
Above the wailing of the rain.

Ledwidge joined the Enniskillen Fusiliers and fought in Gallipoli, Salonica and France. It was while helping to mend a road near Ypres that a shell exploded and killed him on July 31st 1917.

Both James and Henry died in the war; Edward, much to his mother's delight, came home, but the joy was shortlived. James Searles was a member of the Royal Munster Fusiliers and was a handsome man in uniform. He was killed in that fierce battle at Gallipoli on 25 April 1915 where so many soldiers were massacred by the Turks. Eric Bogle, a Scotsman who emigrated to Australia in 1969, tells it better than anybody. He wrote what is arguably the most famous anti-war song in history, 'Waltzing Matilda':

And how well I remember that terrible day,
How our blood stained the sand and the water.
And how in that hell that they call Suvla Bay
We were butchered like lambs to the slaughter.

Henry had served in the 6th Dragoon Guards South Irish Horse Division. He was stationed at Lille in France. Having fought bravely throughout the war, on 1 January 1919 he died of the pneumonia he had developed while recovering from gunshot wounds.

Edward returned home in 1918 but there was no triumphant welcome home to nationalist Ireland in the wake of the 1916 rising for those boys who had fought so bravely and survived this bloodbath. Thomas Kettle, a former nationalist MP who was killed at the Somme, put it aptly when he said of the leaders of the 1916 rising: 'These men will go down in history as heroes and martyrs and I will go down, if I go down at all, as a bloody British officer.' The men returning to nationalist areas from the bloodiest war in history met with grudging acceptance at best, or hostility or even physical violence. Either way they were forgotten in a sort of national amnesia. There was not much work in Bandon for Edward so, as a trained soldier, he joined the Free State army. On his second day of duty he was shot three miles from his home down on the Innishannon Road. His death, so close to home, with a body she could see buried, made his death much more of a reality for Mrs Searles.

The picture of Edward did not hang with those of Henry and James in the front parlour of the Searles' home because Mrs Searles could not bear that much pain. Edward's death was the final straw for this lady brought so low by grief. The great joy of his safe return was shattered by his unfortunate death so close to home.

The Bandon War Memorial Committee located Henry's grave in Lille's Southern Cemetery and placed three white crosses there to mark the deaths of the three brothers. What a comfort it must have been to the Searles family to now know that their sons would be remembered.

After their mother's death, the Searles' home in Boyle Street where the youngest boy, Phil, lived with his sister, Annie, was left untouched in memory of their brothers who died. Their pictures hung in the front parlour until the house was recently sold after Phil's death at the grand old age of ninety-two. No doubt they will always be treasured by Phil's son, Paddy, and his family.

17

The Musician's Tale

In a town which has had so many musicians many would agree that Saxy Dan has brought more pleasure to the people of Bandon in recent years than any other musician in living memory. This quiet and unassuming man is a real ambassador for the town, maintaining and upholding old fashioned values and gentlemanly behaviour.

Born in 1937, Dan was the third of four children. He remembers that in those days, the pre-playpen days, little children learning to walk were put in a tea chest for safety. He recalls the Christmases and the excitement of waiting for Santa Claus and the stocking filled with fruit, nuts and chocolate. He joined the other boys to go out with the wren on St Stephen's Day where they would dress up, take a holly bush and go from house to house singing, 'The wren, the wren, the king of all birds, St Stephen's day he got caught in the furze.'

Dan's family had a small holding near the old site of Allman's Distillery, where they kept three cows, three pigs and a brood of chickens. Dan remembers bringing a clocking hen to the landlady of the KB, who also kept chickens for a time. He also remembers the sad story of the little piggy who nearly didn't make it to market: 'Mother had sold a pig, so it had to be taken to the railway station to be transported to the buyer, who would have bought pigs from other farmers as well. This sad little pig was driven up Boyle Street and Shannon Street by a popular drover who beat the pig so hard that the buyer would only pay half the agreed price. The poor pig's back was red, raw; all the meat was on the stick.'

As a schoolboy Dan spent his holidays on Galvin's farm in Curranure; his mother felt he would be in the fresh air and away from the influence of 'corner boys' as the youngsters who stood on Bandon bridge or hung around street corners with little to do were called. It was quite customary for parents to send their children to family or friends in the country where they would thin beet, feed the chickens and help with the harvest. TB was rampant in Ireland at that time and the parents also felt that plenty of fresh air, together with a diet of fresh, wholesome, home produced food and milk straight from the cow would prevent their offspring from contracting the disease. Many of the pubs at the time burned sulphur candles to fumigate their premises from such airborne viruses.

Dan loved the threshing: that time of year when the harvest was saved to see the farmer through the winter. It was an event that could last for days and men from the town would go to the country to help. A 'firkin', a small barrel containing eight gallons of porter, would be procured from one of the pubs in town to reward the helpers. If it was a big threshing, a 'kil', as the big barrel consisting of sixteen gallons was called, would be bought. The threshing was judged by the amount of porter provided so there was always a 'good' threshing and a 'bad' threshing. The helpers invariably chose to work at the 'good' threshing, which left the meaner farmers with fewer helpers who had to work doubly hard for less porter!

Johnny O'Mahony of Curranure was renowned for the quality of his threshing. He was the milkman for the eastern end of town and was a lovely gentleman. Dan recalls the porter flowing freely, the dancing continuing into the small hours, the chaff from the corn flying out of the turn-ups in the men's trousers and sparks flying off the floor from their hobnailed boots. The women who came to help the farmer's wife with the catering would be dressed up in their best bibs for the occasion while the men would be clad in their old clothes all dusty and sweaty from the hard day's work.

When Dan was sixteen, like many young Bandon boys he joined the FCA, *Forsa Cosanta Aitiúil* or, as it was known locally, 'the Free Clothes Association'. This was an organisation similar to the home guard in Britain – made famous by the programme 'Dad's Army'. The main reason why many of the boys joined the FCA was for the annual trips to the training camps at Collins Barracks, Kilworth or Spike Island, in the days when holidays away from home were beyond their reach. Woken by the *reveille* at seven o'clock every morning, they spent their days marching, training and 'getting to know' their guns: 303 Royal Enfield rifles. They could go out in the evenings to the cinema or a dance but they had to be back to barracks by midnight. Dan says he 'only joined to get the coat'. The members were supplied with a uniform, the most important piece of which was the coat made of frieze material – a strong woollen fabric, tough and hairy, but very warm. It became an eiderdown in many homes including the Kilmichael Bar.

The Bandon FCA had a pipe band which was very much part of the town's life during the 1950s. Dan joined and thus learned to play the bagpipes. His teacher, Jacksy Mahony, was another well-known Bandonian who had been in the army during the Emergency. Corny Looney was the staff major; Dansy Mahony played the big drum; while other neighbours, Terry and Francis Whelton, were side drummers and their cousin, Finbarr Nash, played the pipes. Barry Ellis and three of his brothers also formed part of this band: Jimmy, Liam and Donie played the pipes and Barry played the kettle-drum.

When Saxy Dan left Warner's Lane School, which he moved to after St Fintan's, he went immediately to work in the building trade. He worked by day and attended the technical school in Kilbrogan Hill by night to learn the skills of his trade. Building has remained his day job ever since.

During his childhood Dan never had either singing or music lessons, nor did he own an instrument. When he attended

Miss Mehigan's School (later St Fintan's) he managed to get 'noise' out of a mouth organ, graduated to a comb and then moved on to that most popular of Irish instruments, on which James Galway started his music career – the penny whistle. He also spent many happy hours on the roads of Ballylangly, Monarone and Clashafree listening to and imitating birdsong. He can distinguish the song of the various birds and it is a delight to hear him whistle the tune to 'If I Were a Blackbird'.

The first time he ever saw or heard the saxophone was at the circus. The circus formed the best entertainment of the year and Dan looked forward to its arrival. He was only six or seven years old when he saw his first one. Fossett's and Duffy's circuses visited Bandon annually during the 1940s and 1950s and into the 1960s. These events caused great excitement among the young people in the town who would follow the parade down to Donovan's field, in the early days and later to Quinlan's field in Boyle Street. Dan recalls that as a small child he helped to erect the one pole tent in his parents' field in the Mill Road. The colour, the spectacle and particularly the music played by the circus band, appealed to his creative soul and made a deep impression on him.

Like many other young boys of his time, he listened to Joe Loss and Louise Armstrong on the wireless. However, there is no substitute for live music and soon Dan was involved in the prolific music scene in Bandon in the 1950s – the era of the big band sound. When he was seventeen or eighteen he got his first saxophone with the help of his mother who recognised his extraordinary talent. He hasn't stopped playing since.

The 'platform' was the popular dance floor of the 1940s and 1950s; the 'nursery' of many budding musicians. It was a patch of concrete at a crossroads where the young people of the time cycled every Sunday evening during the summer months to dance until midnight. Then they cycled home again. Bandon was well supplied with such platforms: Clasha-free, Rices Road, Tinkers Cross, Pedlars Cross, Meelin and Harbour View. Crowds of young people gathered at these venues and they each had their share of musical talent. Jerry Donovan of Ballylangly – a regular of the KB – played the melodeon, as did another stalwart, Jerh Lehane, the singer of 'Lovely Maggie May'. According to Dan the melodeon was the first traditional Irish musical instrument.

The town hall, which reputedly had the best dance floor in the country, started life as a private house. It was built in 1790 by brewery owner, George Cornwall and the addition of an assembly room in 1862 turned it into a town hall. It has always been administered by a trust. The greatest bands of the era came there: Maurice Mulcahy, Clipper Carlton, Jimmy Wiley and Mick Delahunty, who always played for the FCA dances. Dances were also held at the Devonshire Arms Hotel, now an apartment block. The Allin Institute no longer holds dances but it is still used as a meeting hall. The boys' club has been demolished. Many dinner dances still take place in the Munster Arms Hotel however.

During his late teens and twenties, Dan played music three or four nights a week with the Ritz Showband, usually on a Thursday, Friday and Sunday. Saturday was confession and bath night and for many it was the senna pod tea night as well, so youngsters were purged inside and outside. Fasting from midnight was necessary for those who wished to receive communion on Sunday morning so everybody had to be tucked up in bed by the witching hour.

Dan travelled the county playing in the Ritz Showband for twelve years from when he joined in 1958. During this time, while playing in Kerry Pike, he met his wife, Margaret. They married in 1963 and had four children, three boys and one girl. His son, Anthony, who emigrated to Australia, is making music there playing bass guitar in a band; and his son, Gerard, plays the keyboard. Sadly tragedy struck Dan and his family at a young age: Margaret died suddenly at the age of forty-five, leaving him with his four children ranging in ages from eleven to twenty-two. It certainly cannot have been easy for any of them.

Dan loves the saxophone and nobody can compete with him. He believes it is the instrument closest to the human voice in its versatility. As well as playing the melodeon and mouth organ he has a fine singing voice. No gathering or party is complete without him.

Phil saw him clear the stage of a group of young musicians at her brother, Barry's, birthday party in Dublin a few years ago. There were several requests from the old Bandonians for

Dan to play the saxophone. The group were amused by this and eventually thought they'd indulge the auld fella. Well, the youngsters were gob-smacked. Suddenly the whole party was up and dancing and they continued until about three o'clock in the morning. The group of young musicians skulked off home around eleven. It was a memorable night.

His music has been enjoyed on the British mainland where he has played with several other Bandon musicians in Bude, Cornwall, to raise money for the lifeboats. The memorable busking trip to Bath is no doubt still remembered by the residents of that Roman city whom they entertained royally while raising money for B–HOC, the group who fundraise for the provision of the hyper-baric oxygen chamber in Bandon, only one of two towns in Ireland which provide such a service. He was accompanied on that occasion by Paddy Downey, Joe McLaughlin, Aiden Rourke, John (Jack) Doyle, Jerry Walsh and Gerard Quirke and several other non-playing assistants, including the indomitable Liam Deasy whose brainchild the chamber is. Dan's charity work is legendary; he shares his talent generously and freely. No is not a word that features in his extensive vocabulary. His faithful saxophone and melodeon travel with him in his reliable red Opel 'just in case' a session might break out.

With his ever-ready smile and his old-fashioned sense of fun, Dan is known and loved by one and all.

18

THE GARDA'S TALE

The first members of the Garda Síochána disembarked from the S.S. *Lady Bandon* in Cork after a day's sailing from Dublin. They spent a few days resting in Moore's Hotel and were then dispersed throughout the principal towns of Co. Cork. They arrived in Bandon on 11 November 1922 and immediately took over the RIC barracks in South Main Street. Bandon's quota was one sergeant and four gardaí: Sergeant Michael McInerney, Garda Patrick Costello, Garda James Lynch, Garda Edward Ryan and Garda Michael Ryan.

Soon the Bandonians were calling the young gardaí 'goslings' and they maintained that they were using the long arm of the law to escort young ladies up and down South Main Street. It must have been difficult for these early recruits to cope with Ireland's innate distrust of the law and their need to break it. When the *ban-gardaí* became popular in Ireland, yes, you've guessed, they were called '*Garda Sicíní*'.

To the publicans of the town a garda's reputation depended on how he treated them. The 'good' gardaí did not interfere with the publican's livelihood, but the 'bad' ones targeted them on a regular basis. James Lynch was such a peace-loving garda that he became known as Ghandi. He was also considered one of Bandon's best detectives and got all his information in pubs. A pub could be compared to a university in those days – anything one needed to know could be learned there! Information was given to Ghandi because the publicans trusted him: he was not over zealous in raiding them. However, any garda who had a reputation for tormenting the drinking public would either be misinformed or not informed at all.

To survive after-hours drinking, a man had to be an all round athlete: he needed to be able to climb, jump, run and crawl, all with a glass in his hand. The fine for those found on the licensed premises was a half a crown – the cost of three pints! There is a story told about a zealous garda who came to raid a pub and found Ghandi on the premises.

'What are you doing here?' demanded the raiding garda.

'Raiding the pub,' responded the quick thinking Ghandi.

The pub-raiding garda would often have the effrontery to advise the publican or his wife how to run their business. This could be a lengthy process and the advice would continue while the drink kept coming. Meanwhile, the customers might be freezing to death on a roof or in a back lane waiting for the 'all clear'. One headline in the *Southern Star* in the 1950s read: 'Man in bed – waiting for Charlie'. This followed a raid on a pub in which the punters had run upstairs and got into beds. The garda went up the stairs and on throwing back the bedclothes found a man in bed with his boots on.

'What are you doing there?' asked the garda.

'Waiting for Charlie,' came the unfortunate reply. Charlie was the owner of the pub!

Deasy's in North Main Street was raided one night and the men dispersed into the yard. Jim Deasy kept pigs and one man decided to jump into the pigsty. The garda shone a flash-lamp into the sty and saw the man crouching behind a big sow.

'What are you doing there?' asked the garda.

'I'm an invited guest,' replied the found-on.

The Munster Arms Hotel was raided on one occasion while Judge Crotty was on the premises. He was quickly ushered into the 'cold room' while the other men were 'caught' in the main bar. This resulted in a court appearance where the assembled company and Mary Mullins the landlady appeared in front of the good judge. The fine at this time was half a crown for the found-ons and seventeen and six for the publican. This was before the draconian laws of endorsements on the licence appeared when after-hours drinking became quite a serious matter. If a publican was caught three times he could then lose his licence and of course, his livelihood. On this occasion the judge fined the landlady thirty shillings and the customers five shillings a man: 'So that I would not be seen to be lenient to a pub in which I drink myself,' pronounced the judge.

Petty crime was only in its infancy in the 1940s and 1950s. Often the gardaí would deal with matters themselves rather than bother Judge Crotty with minor offences; furthermore, they wanted to avoid giving some poor young lad or lass a criminal record. This seemed a good policy and it certainly worked. The young would-be criminal would get a good telling off from the garda and then be taken home to his parents where he got another row or maybe a good belting. Of course, if the head teacher or the nuns discovered any of your misdemeanours you really were in trouble and you would be watched like a hawk until you were back on the straight and narrow. With gardaí, parents and teachers all singing from the same hymn sheet children didn't have a hope of embarking on a life of crime.

Poitín-making and salmon poaching were the two main crimes of the period – neither of which seemed much of a crime. Who can own the rivers? The bounty of the rivers belonged to all. People even sang about them: 'Only our rivers run free'. As much as the people of Bandon loved their earl they believed that neither the river nor the woods belonged to him. They had a point: the great Chief Seattle thought the same when the American government tried to move the Indians off their land:

How can you buy or sell the sky, the warmth of the land?
The idea is strange to us.
If we do not own the freshness of the air and the sparkle of

the water: how can you buy them?

Every part of the earth is sacred to my people.

The ancient Gael had the same notion: the land does not belong to us, rather we belong to the land. The landlady of the KB was in agreement with these wise ancestors. She brought her children up on a diet of 'poached' salmon – a good brain food. It also provided the fisherman with a ready market for the bounty bestowed on them by the river Bandon – reputed to be one of the best salmon rivers in the country. Jack Mahony's brother, Mattie, often regaled the assembled company in the KB with tales of shooting salmon as they leaped up high at the weir. The water bailiff was responsible for policing the river and one morning he opened his door to find a salmon's head pinned to it with a note attached saying, 'Where were you when I was caught?'

No doubt there were good salmon in some garda households as well – perhaps Mac might know! John McInerney, or Mac as he is called, is an honorary member of the KB family and no O'Mahony gathering is complete without him. He barely escaped being a found-on on that unfortunate occasion when his father raided and 'caught' the KB. He managed to escape through the wicket gate about ten minutes before his dad knocked on the front door and declared: 'Guards on public house duty.'

Mac's father, Cornelius (Con) McInerney was born in Tulla, Co. Clare in 1906. He joined the garda síochána in 1926, when the force was still in its infancy. He did his training in the garda depot in the Phoenix Park, in the days before the depot was opened at Templemore. His first posting was to Rosscarbery: a nice, rural beat in a beautiful part of West Cork and it was there that he met the lovely Maisie McDonald. They married sometime later and had four children: a son and three daughters, John, Claire, Pauline and Ita. The latter married Diarmuid O'Donoghue, son of that great historian and headmaster of St Patrick's Boys' School, Liam O'Donoghue. Liam's contribution to the promotion of all things gaelic in the town is without parallel. John (Mac) is the only boy of the family. Con's garda career spanned over forty-two years, all of it spent in Co. Cork. Bandon was his last posting and he retired in 1968. He continued to take an active part in the life of the town until his death in 1974.

Sergeant Bill Leahy, a colleague of Garda McInerney, was responsible for 'weights and measures' – making sure that all measuring equipment was corrct and that the public were not being cheated in any way. He lunched in the KB each day during the working week so the landlady had to make sure that all her measures were in order! He was a nice, gentle soul, incapable of raiding a pub. Another colleague was Sergeant Cahill, who had come to Bandon from Ballineen. He had four daughters. Pat, the youngest girl, was a friend of Phil's so a lot of time was spent to-ing and fro-ing between the KB and the Cahill home in Casement Road. All four Cahill girls emigrated to England at a young age. Mrs Cahill was an elegant and charming lady, always beautifully dressed and with a kind word for everybody. She lived to a great age, spending the latter part of her life in St Michael's Home.

Back then, every house would have a bottle of poitín, that rare old mountain dew which has been made in Ireland since the days when Noah was a boy. It is part of our culture but it caused a lot of problems during the Troubles. The RIC, in their search for a poitín still, would sometimes discover a cache of weapons which they would then confiscate. Some publicans have been known to mix poitín – which is colourless – with whiskey. This is a very dangerous thing to do because 'bad' poitín could cause a man's death or keep him drunk for days. Most people kept it for medicinal purposes or put it in the Christmas cakes and puddings to enhance the flavour. They were very particular about where they procured it and miles would be travelled to find a reputable poitín maker. Many a bottle has crossed the Irish Sea labelled as holy water – no wonder the British customs officers considered the Irish such a religious race!

Poitín punch was part of the New Year's Eve celebrations in the KB where the landlady would make it for her faithful customers. No cold or flu bug would dare land on a person who was insulated with this powerful medicine; hot water in a warm glass, cloves, honey, lemon and a glass of good poitín ensured a winter free of colds. Thomas Crean, that intrepid seafarer, tells a story of a year when the publican made the punch and was rather too heavy-handed with the good stuff, causing a great deal of inebriation. Thomas, who had a new suit for Christmas, had to crawl up Foxes Street on his hands and knees to get home, ruining the knees of his new trousers. Maureen was not pleased and who could blame her?

Now that poaching and poitín-making are obsolete and after-hours drinking is a thing of the past, how do the gardaí 'amuse' themselves? Thankfully, the gardaí are now much more integrated into the community, seen as friends and are no longer viewed with the historical distrust of the 1940s and 1950s. The increase in the Irish crime rate certainly makes the job of the gardaí much more dangerous. We have moved a long way from the days of the local garda arriving on his bike or on foot and when the highlight of his week was catching a publican who was making an old penny on a pint, or catching some fisherman with a large family to feed stealing a salmon from the landlord's river.

19

THE EARL'S TALE

The Bernards were Normans who accompanied William the Conqueror to England in 1066. Clearly their descendants distinguished themselves as soldiers of the king and queen because when Queen Elizabeth I planted Munster with English landowners and tenants Francis Bernard was one of the beneficiaries. Originally he was one of Phane Beecher's tenants – the owner of Castle Mahon – but he was later in a position to buy the castle from Phane's granddaughter and her husband in 1639.

Phane Beecher, founder of the colony at Bandon, obeyed his queen's instructions to the letter. Allegedly, he is the only one in the area who did so, which is why Bandon became such a strong Protestant stronghold. He was offered 547,628 acres of land on which to settle 20,000 English families at a rent of a couple of pennies per acre. Beecher set about this task with fervour and soon no Irish person owned or rented an inch of land on either side of the Glaslyn River – as the Bandon River was called in those times. For his efforts, he was given Castle Mahon, the O'Mahony stronghold which had been built around 1375 by Dermod Mahony, who came south from the clan stronghold at Castlenaleact. The O'Mahonys were the kings of Munster and could trace their origins back to Olioll Olum, king of Munster, who died in ad 234. St Finbarr, patron saint of Cork, is alleged to have been born on the old Iron Age fort on which Castle Mahon was built.

Cnogher (Conor) O'Mahony had supported the earls of Desmond in the Munster risings and lost not only his young life but also his land. All 14,000 acres of his land along both sides of the Glaslyn River were given to Phane Beecher by the queen of England on 30 September 1588. She ordered him to build houses for ninety-one families. The lands were to be given to English Protestants; the queen no longer wanted to have the trouble she had had with the earls of Desmond who had become more Irish than the Irish themselves.

The colonists arrived by ships in Kinsale harbour and made their way along the bridle path past Downdaniel castle, along the northern bank of the river Glasslyn, to the ford a few yards west of the bridge at Castle Mahon. Many of the men had brought their families with them. According to George Bennett, in his excellent *History of Bandon*, wolves still roamed the heavily wooded areas and of course, the natives were 'a fierce, savage people who claimed the land as their own'.

Among the settlers we read such names as Bernard, Baldwin, Bennett, Beamish, Carey, Deane, Griffith, Giles, Hales, Kingston, Perrott, Smith and Tanner; names still to be found in Bandon today. These first settlers were shocked to find a wild uncultivated stretch of land leading nowhere – bogs and woodland – they described it as a 'harbour to rebels, thieves and wolves'. They were hardworking people and within forty years they had cleared the land and built the town, turning the valley of the Bandon river into the fertile land it is today.

Captain William Newce distinguished himself at the Battle of Kinsale and was given a stretch of land to the north of the river. He wanted to build a town where the village of Newcestown now stands, but after an attack by the Crowley clan he abandoned that idea and instead developed the land near the river which became known as the 'Manor of Coolfada', according to Paddy Connolly in his great book – *Bandon – 400 Years of History*. The first provost of the new town of Bandon Bridge was Captain Sir William Newce.

The native Irish were not at all happy with this situation and immediately began a campaign of guerrilla warfare against the settlers who in their view had stolen their land. No Irish person was allowed to live within the town walls. The edict, 'No papist inhabitant shall be suffered to dwell within the town', was a matter of policy rather than prejudice according to the author of *Seasonable Advice*. It was a necessary support for the fledgling colony to which the Irish were extremely hostile.

The fifth Francis Bernard was created baron of Bandon Bridge and in 1794 he was made Viscount Bernard. Later, in 1800, he was given the title of first earl of Bandon as a reward for his efforts in having the Act of Union passed.

Percy Ronald Gardiner Bernard, (better known as 'Paddy Bandon' or 'the Abandoned Paddy') the first earl's great grandson, became the fifth and last earl of Bandon. Born in 1904, in Gillingham, Kent, he was educated at Berkshire College and at the Royal Air Force College in Cranwell, Lincolnshire. Having been commissioned by the RAF in 1929 as part of the 216 bomber squadron he headed for the Middle East in 1931. In 1933, he married Maybel Elizabeth Playfair in Nairobi. They had two daughters: Jennifer Jane and Francis Elizabeth.

After a stint as a flying instructor at the RAF staff college in 1938, he went on to command the 82 bomber squadron during the Second World War. Percy became one of the most distinguished officers of the Second World War; a war historian once wrote: 'Lord Bandon and his group made air history.' Lord Bandon's 224 were in the thick of the air-strikes which greatly helped in the decisive defeat of the Japanese in Burma. He was one of the first RAF officers to be awarded the DSO while serving in France in 1940. He also had the unusual distinction of being appointed to the United States army air force and being awarded the American DC and bronze medal. His courage and leadership qualities in the Far East are best remembered by historians and by his own officers and men. The 224 group performed amazing achievements.

The beaufighters of the 224 group created the world's long distance record when they carried out a series of air strikes at Tavoy on the Tenasserim Coast in South Burma; the flight distance was more than 1,300 miles. These aircraft were involved in a sea blockade maintained from the air. The port of Rangoon, the Irrawaddy delta and the waterways around Henzada were virtually useless to the Japanese as a supply route. Whenever the Japanese attempted to enter these waterways, their heavily laden convoys were wiped out by Lord Bandon's beaufighters.

In 1943, he and his wife, Maybel Elizabeth, divorced. A short time later he met Australian born Lois Olive Russell in Burma and they married in 1945. In 1955, he was appointed commander-in-chief of the second tactical air force with the acting rank of air marshal. The appointment carried with it the NATO post of commander, second allied tactical air force. He was one of the RAF officers involved in the organisation of the famous 'fly pasts', now a familiar sight at so many British state occasions; the first fly past was a feature of the coronation of the present queen. He retired to Bandon in 1963.

Lord Bandon, his wife and daughter, Lady Jennifer, lived in the bungalow beside the ruined castle in Bandon where he enjoyed fishing and shooting with the locals. He was a convivial man who took a keen interest in local affairs and was a popular figure in the town. He was loved for his great sense of humour and for his charity work; he was chairman of the council of the Victoria Hospital, Cork. He gave part of his land to the local golf club who were able to increase the golf course from a nine- to an eighteen-hole course. He was also an active member of the Bandon Game Protection Association and the local Anglers Association.

He died in February 1979 and his funeral was arranged for 3 p.m. on Saturday, 10 February. Billy Johnson, a former resident of Foxes Street and a veteran of the old IRA, was due to have his funeral mass at 3 p.m. the same day. Both men were receiving religious and military honours from their respective churches and governments. Mr Johnson's funeral was to take place in St Patrick's Catholic church and Lord Bandon's in St Peter's Church of Ireland. The funeral in St Peter's was delayed however as the congregation awaited the arrival of the British military attaché in his state car. After a wait that seemed too long church wardens Billy Good and Fergus Applebe were sent by the bishop to track down the air force gentlemen, only to find them in attendance at Mr Johnson's funeral. Having asked for instructions in the town they were directed to the wrong funeral!

Lady Jennifer inherited her father's estates but not the title. Her mother, the countess of Bandon, whose father hailed from Ennis, Co. Clare, lived to the great old age of one hundred and two. She received telegrams and gifts from the president of Ireland, Mrs Mary McAleese and from Queen Elizabeth II of England. She died peacefully in October 1999 having survived her beloved earl by twenty years.

20

THE TALE OF THE
DRAY DRIVER

In 1955, the newly built housing estate at the top of Foxes Street, Ardán na nÓglaigh, opened its doors. Thirty-six families moved in, among them Jerome Donovan and his family.

Jerome was born on 12 August 1897 in Kilbarry near Dunmanway and moved to Bandon with his parents when he was a boy of fourteen or fifteen. His father managed farms for people who had outside farms and the young Jerome would help him with his work. He often told the story of how, in 1915, while he was living on a farm in Skeaf, Timoleague, he was sent by his father to a field some distance from the dwelling house to assist with the calving of a cow. All of a sudden he heard two loud explosions. He looked out to sea and saw what looked like a skyscraper sticking up out of the water: what he was witnessing was the sinking of the *Lusitania*. Years later when he first saw a skyscraper it reminded him of that terrible sight from south of the Old Head of Kinsale on that fatal day.

He went to work for Beamish and Crawford in Watergate Street and lived in the lodge at the foot of Kilbeg Hill. He and his colleague, Maurice Sexton, drove the brewery horse and dray delivering barrels of porter to the many pubs in town. He interrupted this service in his younger days by going to Wales where he worked for four years in a coalmine in the famous Rhonnda Valley. His plan was to emigrate to Canada and join the mounties but the friend with whom he planned to go failed to arrive at the train station. So the young Jerome returned home to Bandon where he remained for the rest of his life.

When he was forty years old, he married Mary Ann (Molly) O'Connell, a farmer's daughter from Gloun South, near his own birth place at Kilbarry. They raised a family of two boys and four girls. Gerard, the eldest, still resides in the family home in Ardan, a fine gentleman like his father. He had to leave school to become the family bread winner for seven years when his father received an injury at work: a crib from a lorry had fallen on his back, causing so much damage that Jerome had to have major back surgery. He spent twelve months in the Orthopaedic Hospital in a plaster cast, followed by six months lying on his front and a further six months on his back. When he was eventually discharged from hospital he had to learn to walk again. It was seven years before he was fit enough to return to work. Two of Jerome and Molly's daughters have sadly died: Eleanor, who emigrated to Los Angeles, died in 2001; and Kathleen, who emigrated to Adelaide died during the 1990s. The two younger girls, Mary and Anne, are both married and living in Ireland. Donie, who transported Phil's trunk to Milford Haven when she emigrated, lived in England for some time but has now returned to his native Ardan.

During the Second World War Jerome worked with a pair of horses delivering beer to the pubs in Castletownbere. No lorries could be used because of petrol rationing and those which were used were fuelled by charcoal. The brewery had a depot in Bantry but Jerome's base was still in Bandon so he had to take a load from Bandon to Bantry – no mean journey. He often had to stay in Bantry overnight and deliver to Castle-townbere the next day. When he got to Cooleragh Hill, be-tween Glengarriff and Castletownbere, he would remove half the load at the bottom of the hill, take the remaining half up to the top, unload it and then return to pick up the other half. Then he would continue on his way with the full load – this was out of consideration for the horses. The last Beamish dray horse was called Captain and he was kept in the brewery until his death, to be spoilt by the men there.

In the Bandon of the 1950s the day was punctuated by the brewery hooter which roused children from their beds at five to eight, warning the workers that they had five minutes before clocking in for work. It boomed out again at eight o'clock. It was the same procedure at lunchtime – five to one and one o'clock. The workers departed for lunch and an hour later they returned to the same blast. The girls of Shannon Street knew that if they had not arrived home by the second hooter at one o'clock they would not get back to school on time for the afternoon session at one-thirty. The convent girls had only three-quarters of an hour for lunch; Mr Hamilton was much more realistic and allowed his boys an hour's break. Coming home for lunch was not such a good idea as the girls had to run all the way home and back and the return journey was entirely uphill. The next warnings boomed out at twenty-five past and half past five.

Jerome was a keen gardener and as well as cultivating his own garden in Ardan he, like most of the residents adjacent to Spring Lane, had allotments where they grew vegetables. Gerard recalls picking spuds on his father's plot along with other children from the area who would be doing likewise. Every inch of space was used for the growing of this food which was so important to feed their families. If any man was ill or unable to manage his own plot the neighbours would get together and do it for him. This was a time of great neigh-bourliness when people helped each other in so many ways. Communities were built up in adversity; Bandonians had seen such hard times while the auxiliaries and the black and tans were based in the town. Today, a bypass runs through the allotment where Gerard and his father, along with many other families, dug spuds.

Jerome's son, Gerard, also worked for Beamish and Craw-ford and did his drinking in the KB. He is a keen huntsman and fisherman; the KB was home to quite a few fishermen. One day one of the fishermen, after an excellent day's fishing, arrived at the bar to display the beautiful 'bar of silver' he had caught: a beautiful ten or twelve pound spring salmon. He placed it under his chair and engaged in the general banter peculiar to the pub. People came and went all admiring the beautiful fish. One of the arrivals was accompanied by a dog and the next person to view the fish observed that half of it had been eaten. All eyes settled on the dog who beat a hasty retreat with his owner. Gerard joined the part time fire service in 1963 and continued to serve the community until his retirement as station officer in 2005.

According to Jerry Desmond, there has been a fire service in Bandon since the eighteenth century. Until 1939 the engine used was a hand pump worked by twelve men, six at each side, pumping up and down. In the event of a fire it had to be pushed around by hand or pulled by horses; the horses could be commandeered from any farmer passing the road. Eventually they acquired an old pump from the town commissioners and Roddy Macklin – the father of fire-fighting in Bandon – with the assistance of another mechanic, fitted a Ford petrol engine which could be placed on a trailer and pulled by a vehicle. The pump could then be placed by an open water source – a pond, lake or river. The hose would run from there to the site of the fire. In those days, according to Gerard Donovan, it was not unusual to run a line of hose for half a mile or more. This continued until the county council established the fire service on a more permanent basis in 1945 with Roddy Macklin as station officer and John Hayes as his assistant. In 1950, the first fire station was opened in South Main Street. It remained there for thirty-seven years until it was moved to its present site on the West Cork Lane.

Drinking has been part of the Irish culture since the dawn of time and beer has been brewed in Bandon since the eighteenth century; at one time the town could boast of three breweries. As brewing by individual pubs decreased, the official brewing of beer grew – much to the advantage of George Cornwall's brewery in Watergate. George's sons, who felt they had made their money, sold the brewery to T.K. Sullivan who sold it to Allman, Dowden and Co. The Allman family were renowned for the quality and excellence of their projects so it was no surprise when they set about modernising the brewery, building a new malt house and bottling plant and increasing its output by adding two new ales and a mineral water to its range of products. John Walsh, who represented Beamish and Crawford in the town, bought the brewery in 1913.

Beamish and Crawford had a brewery in South Main Street Cork so they never brewed in Bandon. While the premises in Watergate have always been called a brewery, the beer was transported to Bandon where it was bottled and redistributed throughout West Cork and Kerry. The famous 'Little Norah' mineral water was manufactured and bottled in Bandon. It was one of the most important employers in the town in the 1940s and 1950s. The participation of the

Beamish and Crawford floats in the carnivals and parades is legendary; they seemed to have the most talented staff in the town. In 1962, Beamish and Crawford went the way of many indigenous industries and was taken over by Canadian Breweries who closed the Bandon brewery in 1967 and moved the whole operation to Cork. Some of the staff were relocated but many were sadly made redundant and the famous hooter was heard no more.

Jerome retired from Beamish's shortly before the closure of the Bandon Brewery. He became the town's oldest barman for a year or two managing Liam Deasy's pub in the North Main Street. He enjoyed working in his beloved garden and selling the produce, along with plants and shrubs which he had grown, at the mart. He went regularly to the Kilmichael Bar for his pint and chat with his friends. This convivial and hard-working man died at the grand old age of eighty-six.

21

THE TALE OF THE SOLDIER'S WIFE

Jane Burke, that grand old lady who lives in Shannon Street, has been surrounded by army men her whole life, beginning with her father who fought first in the Boer War and then in the First World War. Her four brothers were also army men: Johnny, her eldest brother, joined the British army, fought in the Second World War and spent eighteen years in India; Bob joined the army as a horseman serving in the cavalry division and spent twelve years in India. During their time in India, even though Johnny and Bob were not stationed in the same part of the sub-continent, Johnny would sometimes fly down to south India to see his brother. Jim and Willie joined the navy and sadly Jim was killed during the Second World War at the age of twenty-six. On 8 June 1940, the ship on which he was serving, *HMS Glorious*, was torpedoed 150 miles from the Norwegian coast. He had passed all his exams to become a petty officer and was to be elevated to this post on his return to England but unfortunately he never returned. Jane recalled: 'Minister Brown came down to the house the minute he heard about Jim's death; he was a very good man. We first got the telegram that Jim was missing; my father who was unwell at the time was very distressed, so when we got the telegram telling us Jim was dead, we didn't tell him. Every week after that when he got his pension, he gave my mother half a crown to buy food and send it to Jim, "because," he said, "they starve prisoners of war". He had such a good heart even though he was an invalid.'

Jane's husband, Paddy Burke, from Bruree, Co. Limerick was a sergeant in the Irish army and was stationed in Bandon for quite some time. Their eldest son, Paddy, also joined the army where he had a distinguished career.

Mr Barrett, Jane's father, was a cobbler. He made shoes and sold them on fair days at twelve shillings a pair. All her brothers were trained as cobblers but only Johnny worked at it when he left the army. Jane's sons, Paddy and Willie, both served their time with Johnny but none of them continued with the trade. She recalls the time when Willie went on strike for more money: he walked up and down outside Johnny's house but Johnny only laughed at him and didn't give him his pay increase!

Being directly opposite Foxes Street the Barrett house often fell foul of floods and on very wet days the water would run down the hill and cascade in the front door and out through the back door. To prevent this from happening a low wall was built at the outside of the pavement along the lower end of Shannon Street. Before the building of the wall there was great excitement one day when a jennet, coming too quickly down the hill, his handler failing to control him, ended up in the Barrett's hallway. Another Monday morning the family had a less welcome visitor when a cow from the mart went into the hallway and up the stairs. The poor animal got stuck in the bend of the stairs and couldn't move either up or down!

Jane once told Phil the story of one of her earliest memories from during the War of Independence:

'We were young at the time – Johnny, Willie and myself. We slept on mattresses on the floor at night because of the shooting from the roof of the Devon [the military barracks where the auxiliaries were stationed]. I remember one night when we had to leave the house in Shannon Street. The auxiliaries were looking at the names on the doors; they were going to burn us out. Johnny was the eldest and he took Margaret and Willie on his back down over the railway. We made our way down to Foley's in Ballylangly. Mrs Foley made tea for us and we slept there for the night. My father stayed at home with the dog and came down to get us when it was safe.'

The black and tans and the auxiliary police force were a scourge in almost every Irish town in those uncertain days. Both groups were only answerable directly to the British cabinet so they really had a *carte blanche* to behave as they wished in Ireland. They burned, murdered and beat the Irish population unmercifully and rarely distinguished between men, women and children. The Bandon auxiliaries were stationed at the old Bandon military barracks which later became the Devonshire Arms Hotel and is now a block of apartments. The infamous Essex regiment had as their leader Major Arthur Ernest Percival, who later received the OBE for his 'efforts' in Ireland during that time.

Mrs Barrett, Jane's mother, was accustomed to going out to her back door in the evenings to watch the six o'clock train coming in from the west. Jane tells the following story:

'She liked to see the train come in and sometimes the passengers would wave. One particular evening she fainted when a sniper took a potshot at her from the train and split the stone on the wall beside her. When she came round my father said to her, "you won't go out again" and you may be sure she didn't.'

All the houses had steel or galvanised iron blinds on their windows to protect themselves from ricocheting bullets during the curfew, when either the black and tans or the auxiliaries were randomly shooting in the streets. John Deasy from Shannon Street happened to look out through a hole in the blind on his front window and saw an auxiliary taking a potshot at Barry Ellis' grandmother who had lost her son in the First World War. She was crossing the road opposite her home in Boyle Street after curfew to get a bucket of water.

Now in her nineties Jane still enjoys a joke and has so

many stories to tell. She is a wonderful woman. Like so many of her generation she saw hardship and the breakdown of law and order in her youth – when the RIC were retiring in their droves – but she seemed to be able to go forward with determination and spirit. She certainly is a fine example of the faith and courage of the women of her day – *Mná na hÉireann* – what a legacy they have left us.

22

THE MILLER'S TALE

In Bandon, the name Brennan is synonymous with milling and baking. Most families in the town ate Brennan's bread. Joseph Brennan was an entrepreneur. He set up many businesses all of which were successful. He was regarded as one of Bandon's and West Cork's, most successful business men.

Long before the Shannon electrical scheme he had harnessed the Bandon river and provided electric light for the town. This enterprise was known as 'Bandon Milling and Electric Lighting Co. Ltd' and it continued to illuminate the town until the ESB was established and took over the service.

As well as the mill Joe Brennan established a grocery store in Shannon Street, where bread was baked before the establishment of the bakery. Another of his enterprises was a profitable agency for Murphy's brewery which he administered very successfully by setting up the West Cork Bottling Company. He owned a woollen mill in Bantry and a hotel, the Esplanade, in Courtmacsherry; the Esplanade had been the former dwelling of the earls of Shannon. Added to all this he had an extensive export trade from the mill. He directed and managed all his businesses until he appointed John Murphy as manager at the mill. According to Leon O'Broin in his biography of Joe Brennan Junior, *No Man's Man*, the mill flourished under Murphy's stewardship. Many new processes were patented which were exhibited regularly at the Dublin Spring Show. The mill did a very big trade in oats, which were exported. A fleet of vans delivered Brennan's bread throughout West Cork.

Joseph Brennan married Mary Hickey and they had seven children: four boys and three girls. Two of his sons, Jeremiah and Shaun, joined the British army and took part in the First World War. Sadly Lieutenant Jeremiah Brennan, of the Lancashire Hussars, was killed in France in August 1918. He is buried in St Hilaire cemetery extension, Frevent. Shaun, thankfully, returned safely to Bandon and later managed the mill. Joe, who became chairman of the Irish Currency Commission and governor of the central bank was known in Bandon as 'Joe Pound' because his signature appeared on Irish currency notes from 1928 to 1953. Tom became managing director of the West Cork Bottling Company. Margaret joined the Ursuline Sisters and became Mother Baptist. Nell married Jerry Callanan's father. And Moll, his third daughter, married Colman Donovan, who later became Irish ambassador to the Vatican. The family lived at Hill Terrace but later moved to that beautiful Georgian House, Kilbrogan House, at the top of Kilbrogan Hill.

Mr Brennan suffered greatly during the War of Independence. In 1920, he was refused admission to his own mill as it was being searched by the black and tans. In 1921, his home and the mill were again raided resulting in some damage and the movement of bakery vans was restricted. His son, Shaun, was arrested on suspicion of being involved in the killing of a baker in Ballineen who had been shot as a spy by the IRA. Shaun was asked by the soldiers to take a bread van out to remove the body. He refused and they kept him in prison for three days. Added to all of this the Esplanade hotel was burned down by the IRA because Joseph refused to pay a levy for the purchase of arms. His son, Joe Pound, demanded an enquiry into the raids on the mill and on his home but it never came to pass.

Young Joe Brennan was born on 18 November 1887. He attended the local school until he was thirteen and then went on to Clongowes Wood where he excelled as a student and gained entry into Christ College, Cambridge. There he studied mathematics and classics and won first place in Latin and Greek. In 1911, he became a civil servant: firstly, in the department of customs and excise and then he moved to the chief secretary's office in Dublin Castle. He met Michael Collins during the Truce and was asked to become financial advisor to the group who, led by Michael Collins, went to London in 1921 to negotiate the peace treaty with Lloyd George. Joe, as a senior British civil servant was put in a difficult position, but he agreed to help and he prepared all the necessary financial advice and documentation for the delegation.

Whenever he could get away from his office, Brennan slaved away secretly at this strange assignment and produced eight separate papers, all of which he typed himself for, in what he described as a 'highly dangerous' situation, he could not possibly entrust the work to anyone else.

After the ratification of the Treaty, Dublin Castle was formally handed over to Michael Collins. Collins invited Joe Brennan to set up the Irish Exchequer. Brennan's bakery, which had opened in 1914, was sold to Hosfords in 1960. Early on the fateful morning of 6 May 1968 Brennan's mill went on fire and was totally destroyed. The West Cork Bottling Company closed in 1978. Joseph Brennan provided employment for so many Bandonians over the years that the demise of these businesses was a great blow to the town.

In spite of his amazing business skills and his success, Joseph Brennan was reputedly a quiet, shy man, who refused any public appointments. Neither did he wish to have anything to do with politics because 'he felt there was a lot of trickery involved'. He enjoyed a game of rugby and was a member of the team who won the Munster Senior Cup when that trophy was first put up for competition in 1886. He died at his home on 31 May 1948. He was one of the greatest business men Bandon has ever seen.

23

THE TALE OF BARRY

Although Phil has been friends with Barry Ellis for as long as she can remember, she cannot say when she first met him. He was always part of the life of the KB family. Born on 1 September 1945, he was one of twelve children. He still lives in the family home in Boyle Street with his sister, Peggy and his brother, Anthony.

Barry was a good scholar, interested in school and in books. This is borne out by his fund of knowledge and by his commitment to the War Memorial committee. In collaboration with Billy Good, he edited that excellent book *A Journey of Remembrance* which informs Bandonians of the brave and heroic deeds of so many of the town's young men in international conflicts: the First World War, the Second World War and even in the Boer War.

When Barry graduated from the primary school at Warner's Lane, he attended the vocational school that was then located in Kilbrogan Hill. As well as learning the practical skills of woodwork and metalwork, he continued his study of English, Irish and arithmetic. Unfortunately, coming from a large family, he had to work when seasonal employment was available – thinning vegetables and picking potatoes. This meant that he was prevented from sitting his end-of-year examinations. The result was that he left school with few qualifications.

Barry's first employment during the summer holidays – secured for him by Finbarr Wilmot – involved using a hosepipe to fill tanks with water for the plasterers working on the houses in Ardan in the early 1950s. He was a young lad of about eight or nine at the time. He also did a couple of stints as a drover with Jimmy Deasy, taking cattle to the railway holding yard, a task for which they were well paid, he says.

One of his earliest summer jobs was helping Johnny O'Mahony, the milkman, deliver the milk; firstly in a horse and trap and latterly in the blue van. He remembers people asking him for the 'tuile' for the cat, many of them not having a cat but needing the extra milk for their families in those hard times when money was scarce. In lean times, between his milk rounds, the landlady engaged him as kitchen boy in the KB where he cleaned potatoes and helped generally with washing up and the like, all the time entertaining the other staff with his funny stories.

When he was a mere fifteen or sixteen he went to work for the West Cork Bottling Company. He stayed there until its closure in 1978 when he was transferred with his friend,

Tommy, to the bottling plant in the Kinsale Road – a branch of Murphy's brewery. In June 1854, James Murphy and Co. had bought the site of the Cork Foundling Hospital and set up a brewery there which they named Ladyswell. The company expanded to Bandon in 1896 and set up the West Cork Bottling Company. It was there that Murphy's bottled their porter and made their minerals in association with Joseph Brennan, the miller, who had the Murphy agency in Bandon at the time. From here the company extended into the far reaches of West Cork.

The West Cork Bottling Company – situated where the fire station is now housed – employed nearly a hundred Bandonians at the height of its production. Originally, the goods were transported by rail and horse and dray but with the demise of the West Cork Railway lorries were introduced. The bottling company's lorries could be seen all over Cork county, often with Barry or Tommy on board. Phil often saw the lorries in Kinsale when, as a young nun, she would be going on visitation with an older nun. Sadly she had to keep 'custody of the eyes' and was not allowed to speak with the drivers or helpers whom she knew well. She was quite upset about this but the men seemed to understand convent rules better than she did. They always reported these 'sightings' to the family back at the KB.

Before Barry became a teetotaller, he was a regular at the KB where he enjoyed many a pint and a sing-song. He was one of the key players in the 'outings'. These outings took place for a couple of years until they ran out of steam. From January until August the men paid some money each week into a fund which the landlady held for them so that when the day of the outing dawned all was already paid for. The landlady ordered a bus and about thirty or forty of the regulars, sometimes with their wives, assembled at the bar in the morning, had a few shorts and then set off west.

They always seemed to follow the same pattern: lunch at the West Cork Hotel, Skibbereen and then on to Durrus, where they stopped for a few drinks and a sing-song. The next stop was the West Lodge Hotel in Bantry for their tea, which was quite a substantial affair, not tea and buns or sandwiches as the word tea suggests. They had 'a bit of a dance there', according to Tommy, before starting on the return journey. The last stop was usually in Enniskeane where they spent an hour before getting back to base. Members of the family often participated in this outing.

The name Ellis has always been associated with sport in Bandon. Barry's father, Willy, born in 1904, played hurling and football for Bandon and together with Dr Callanan and Jim Ring, was on the 1929 Bandon team which won the Cork County final. He joined the Irish army on 16 March 1925 and left it in 1934; he returned to the army with many other Bandonians on 24 June 1940 to defend Ireland during the Emergency. He was also a member of the 1928 All Ireland army winning hurling team – the 14th Infantry Battalion of the 6th Brigade. A photograph of this team is displayed in Collins Barracks Museum, Cork and can also be seen in the military archives held at Cathal Brugha Barracks, Dublin. Barry recalls that the Irish soldiers wore the same uniforms as those worn by the soldiers of the First World War. On Willy's discharge from the army in 1946 he worked for various employers in the town but since the work situation was not good he was forced to emigrate to England in the late 1940s. An accident at work damaged his back irreparably and unable to work again, he was forced to return home in the early 1960s. He died on 3 October 1980.

Bandon Workingmen's Society had a fife and drum band in which most of the members were from Shannon Street, Foxes Street and Boyle Street. This group all joined the forces that fought in the First World War and have been mentioned in dispatches for their bravery. Their record has been hailed as the best of any other workingmen's society in the land. The names Searles, Walsh, Crean, Ellis, Wilmot and Canniffe are much in evidence in this role of honour.

Company Sergeant Major James Ellis, Barry's uncle, carved his name on the round tower on the hill overlooking Down-daniel Castle near Innishannon before he went away to war. Sadly, he never returned. He was a member of the 8th Battalion Royal Munster Fusiliers and was recommended for the DCM for bravery. Unfortunately, it is not customary for the British army to decorate people posthumously. He was wounded across the road from St Mary's advanced dressing station, which later became a cemetery – Rudyard Kipling's son is buried there. Sergeant Major Ellis was moved by stretcher to the small French town of Mazingarbe where he died on 14 August 1916 and where he is buried. Barry's grandparents received the following letter from Major Lawrence Roche at the war office, written on Wednesday, 16 August 1916:

Dear Mr Ellis,

I can assure you nothing gave me greater pain than to announce the death in action of your brave son Sgt. Major James Ellis at 1.30 p.m. this morning. I was with him at the end and he had a glorious death. I saw him receive holy communion on Sunday morning and he was in every way prepared to meet his God. He was the most valuable non-commissioned officer I had and I sorely miss him. He was the bravest of the brave and the truest of line.

Yours faithfully,

Lawrence Roche (Major)

Mr Ellis also received a letter from Sergeant Denis O'Brien from Foxes Street who was in the same battalion as James:

Dear Bill,

It is with a sad heart I am sending these few lines to you at the request of your son Jimmy, to whom I was speaking before he died. He got hit while making a raid on the German trenches. I saw some wounded being brought along. I enquired who they were. When Jimmy asked, 'Is that Danny?' I said

'Yes, are you hit?' He said, 'Yes, I am hit badly'. He told the stretcher bearers to let him down a while; I knelt by his side and asked was there anything I could do for him. He said, 'No, but write to my mother and tell her I am gone and not to trouble about me, as I am not afraid to die.' He said no more. He was getting weak. They took him to the dressing station, but he passed away quietly to God at about 2.30 a.m. on Wednesday. He was a good boy and as good a soldier as ever held a rifle and bayonet. We are sorry for him dear Bill, I feel for you and your wife in your trouble, you lost a good son and we lost a good comrade.

Yours in sympathy,

D. O'Brien

Barry Ellis joined the War Graves committee in 1996 and his commitment to it is well documented. Since 1995, he has visited the war graves of France and Belgium annually. The first visit by Bandonians to the graves of their loved ones killed during the First World War took place in 1995, when six members of the Ellis family, Peggy, Georgina, Marion, Ita, Liam and Barry, accompanied by David Sheehan, visited the grave of Sergeant Major James Ellis. The group travelled with Flanders Tours, a travel company set up Colonel Graham Parker, a war veteran who organised tours to the cemeteries. Colonel Parker conducted a prayer service at the graveside for the family. It was a very moving and comforting experience, according to Barry and they were very grateful to Colonel

Parker for making their pilgrimage so memorable. They also visited the graves of David's grandfather and great uncle. Barry now organises trips on behalf of the War Graves commission to the cemeteries where so many of those who died in two world wars are laid to rest. He arranges bus and air travel as well as the accommodation and the tours of the cemeteries. Each itinerary is listed in the book, A *Journey of Remembrance*.

For the eightieth anniversary of the armistice the parade at Ieper in Belgium was led by the three Bandon men, George Duke, Billy Good and Barry, who laid wreaths. Everyone who walked in the parade was given a poppy petal. They walked to the Menin Gate – one of four memorials to those who died in Belgium and have no graves – which commemorates those who fell before 16 August 1917 and bears the names of 54,000 officers and men. The petals were then dropped down through three openings in the roof during the ceremony of remembrance – a most moving sight.

> *They shall grow not old, as we that are left grow old:*
> *Age shall not weary them, nor the years condemn.*
> *At the going down of the sun and in the morning*
> *We will remember them.*

> From 'For the Fallen' by Laurence Binyon

The Island of Ireland Peace Park and Round Tower were opened as part of the eightieth anniversary of Armistice Day celebrations. The stones for the tower came from the workhouse at Mullingar, from where almost 200 young men had joined the British forces. The king and queen of Belgium, the queen of England and the president of Ireland were present at this dedication and honouring of all those from the whole island of Ireland who died in the First World War. The Bandon delegation again played a major role in this event.

During his 1998 visit to Belgium, Barry visited a church which housed peace bells from all over the world. He struck up a friendship with the church caretaker, Albert, who informed him that there was no bell from the Irish republic. On his return home Barry wrote a four page letter to President Mary Robinson outlining all the reasons why the Irish republic should be represented at this place of peace. When Barry returned the following year, there in pride of place in front of the altar was a three foot high bell which had been presented by the people of Ireland. Imagine Barry's pride when Albert singled him out and told the assembled crowd in the church: 'This is the man who got this bell for me.'

Barry has come a very long way since the days he helped in the KB kitchen and delivered milk for Johnny O'Mahony. He is somebody who can be justly proud of himself and the contribution he has made to his local community, whose respect he has gained and where he is loved.

24

THE MILKMAN'S TALE

The buying of a bottle of milk or the 'white stuff' as Jack Charlton calls it, is quite a recent practice. Milk was historically delivered to the door by a milkman. Each milkman had his own area to cover. Bandon was well served since milkmen were located at all the main entrances and exits of the town. Denny Burke from Coolfada and his three handsome sons, Joe, Denis and Kevin, supplied the north side of the town, down as far as the bridge.

These young men ran the gauntlet every morning with hundreds of girls attending school at the convent calling out to them and distracting them from the task of delivering milk. The fact that they didn't spill all the milk is a minor miracle. They made their way down Convent Hill aboard their pony and trap. If the milkmen had reached Kilbrogan Hill by the time the girls saw them, they knew that they were late for school and had to run all the way up Convent Hill. The pony knew exactly where to stop and the milk was transferred from the churns into the big containers from which it was poured into the housewife's jug or sweet gallon. This, of course, was the easy part. The milkman and his family had been up since before dawn and had milked a large herd of cows by hand – in those far off days before milking machines – before setting off to deliver the milk. Most milkmen were on the road by about 8 a.m.

A beautiful herd of cows went past the Kilmichael Bar daily at milking time. They were the property of Mickey Quinlan who lived in Shannon Street. He had a big yard behind his house where he milked the cows. He delivered milk around town but mostly people came to his shop with a jug or gallon and bought milk by the pint. The cows grazed in Quinlan's field which was off Boyle Street, down by the railway – the same field which was visited by the circus every year.

The southside was serviced by Johnny O'Mahony who was born in Killountain. There were eight children in his father, Jeremiah's, family and when his eldest brother inherited the home farm Jeremiah moved to Curranure with his wife and the two-year-old Johnny. They had a further three sons: Jerry, who butchered with Paddy Sweeney in South Main Street, Peter and Michael. The young Johnny took over the milk round from his uncle, John O'Mahony of Clashafree. Both he and Francie Foley, Ballylangly, supplied milk to the southeastern side of town and both delivered to the Kilmichael Bar.

On a visit to Johnny's home recently, in the company of

Pat Wilmot and Dan Donovan, Phil enjoyed his stories of milk deliveries. Johnny joked about Dan keeping his finger in his mouth until he was about twelve years old. Dan took this in good part, retorting: 'There are many who think I should have left it there.' Dan had worked on the farm at Curranure as a young boy and Johnny announced that he only 'came for a good feed'. Dan recalled that 'there was more dancing done in this kitchen than in the Lilac [the popular dance hall in Enniskeane during the showband era of the 1960s]'. Having been offered a drink of whiskey and a cup of tea, Dan and Pat proclaimed they were indeed welcome. Apparently, the tea pot or whiskey bottle was produced if the guests were welcome; if not, neither would be produced and the guests would know that they needed to beat a hasty retreat. On this cold January day both were produced so the welcome was very warm indeed.

Johnny delivered milk in Bandon for thirty years, finishing in 1970. His round included Distillery Road, Boyle Street, Shannon Street, Ardan and Foxes Street with some customers as far afield as Castle Road, North Main Street and Watergate. He graduated from the pony and trap to the blue van but never got into the delivery of bottles. Hard work and the introduction of pasteurisation killed off the business of these hardworking farmers who were, to a large degree, nocturnal to supply their customers with milk for the breakfast.

In 1960, Johnny married his lovely wife, Maureen and they had six children. Their eldest daughter, Eileen, teaches in Kilcoe in West Cork. Dermot manages the farm in Curranure. Ann lives in Dublin and has interests in the well known restaurant chain, O'Brien Sandwiches. Paddy, married to the former mayor of Bandon, Margaret Murphy O'Mahony, lives locally and works for the South of Ireland Petroleum Company. Rose, Paddy's twin sister, having trained as a nurse has now transferred to pastoral care. Their youngest son, J.J., works in the world of finance providing mortgages for house buyers.

Failing health had forced Johnny to give up driving a few years ago and his sons drove him to the Old Still two or three nights a week to share a few pints of the 'black stuff' with him. Phil has been saddened by the news of Johnny's recent death. The passing of this grand old gentleman signifies the speed with which the lives of those who inhabited her childhood and were part of the rich tapestry of the Kilmichael Bar are being snuffed out. Each life is such a unique and such a fragile gift, it behoves us to live it well in the mode of this hard working man who served his community so well. May he rest in peace.

25

The Cook's Tale

As a young girl, Mary Dukelow came from her farm in Durrus – where she had worked briefly for the rector and his family – to work in Miss Beamish's maternity hospital in Bandon in the late 1930s. She was a hard working young girl who enjoyed helping to look after the mothers and their newborn babies. She left when Miss Beamish retired. The hospital was sold to a community of Dominican nuns who changed the name to St Philomena's nursing home. Mary worked in a wool shop until she married Walter Shannon and gave birth to her own two children, Robert and Margaret. Waltie, as he was known, could trace his roots back to the earls of Shannon who owned the Bandon suburb called Irishtown and who were descended from Richard Boyle, the first earl of Cork.

When the landlady of the Kilmichael Bar decided to serve food on mart days, Mrs Shannon came to help cook and serve the food. The KB being the nearest pub to the mart it afforded an ideal opportunity for exploitation. A notice was erected, 'Kilmichael Bar for Dinners and Teas' and the proprietors were in business. Later on, Denny Murphy opened the Old Still which is still there. Daly's from Gloun, near Dunmanway, had the licence for the mart bar and there was also a restaurant on the mart site. Monday, the day of the cattle sale, was the really busy day at the mart; it brought farmers from far and wide and soon the majority of them were dining in the KB. Tuesday was sheep sale day. Wednesday and Saturday were the days when pigs were sold. Most weeks there were four sales held at the Bandon mart and sometimes, on a particularly busy week, there was a sale on a Friday.

The farmers were served good, wholesome, healthy food, naturally organic, nothing fancy and not a lot of variety. Since there were no menus, the choice was take it or leave it. The dinner consisted of: soup and bread; a main course – ham, beef, potatoes, vegetables in season; a desert – seasonal fruit and custard or jelly and ice-cream; all washed down by a cup of Barry's tea and one of Hugh Crowley's buns. Hugh Crowley had a shop in Bridge Street where he baked confectionary. Farmers still talk about the good feeds they had in the KB on mart days.

Soon the lorry drivers were coming in for their meals as well, mostly those transporting beet to the sugar factory at Mallow as their hours were very irregular. This was the situation back in the days before the Glasslyn Road was constructed and everybody who came from the west had to pass through Shannon Street and Boyle Street There were no regular mealtimes – twelve, one, two, or three o'clock. When they came, they got fed, even until nine or ten o'clock at night if necessary. Tail ends of beef were purchased from John Desmond until he retired and then from Tony Jordan. Hams were delivered by Murphy's Evergreen Bacon Company. The meats were boiled in huge saucepans, allowed to cool, then carved when needed. The water from the meat formed the basis for the soup or was used to boil the vegetables, giving them a nice flavour. The scullery was small so the 'house across the yard' was used for boiling the big pots. It was equipped with primuses and gas-rings. The amount of cooking accomplished using such limited equipment was indeed surprising.

Monday being the busiest day of the week extra staff were drafted in – Mrs Falvey, Mrs Collins (John Joe Mahony's sister) and Elsie Ring were some of the regulars. Barry Ellis, with the landlady's children, helped to peel potatoes and wash up. The peeling of spuds was a job hated by all because the task took such a long time. Sometimes the potatoes had to be peeled when hot which was a real trial. Washing up in a confined space wasn't much fun either, especially when everybody seemed to be in such a hurry. After Phil's departure for the convent other staff members were employed. She has vivid memories of Gerald McCarthy from Distillery Road who spoke 'a language which the clergy did not know'. He shopped and cooked for the publican following the landlady's death.

A barman was also engaged for a time and he was a dapper man. One day a couple came to the bar and the man ordered a sherry for his wife. Discovering a fly in the sherry, her husband returned it to the barman who removed the fly and returned the same glass of sherry to the lady! Even in those days it was difficult to get reliable staff. Mary Shannon, a most reliable lady, was horrified by this unhygienic blunder.

Mrs Shannon loved playing cards. Very often, if there were a few stragglers left from the mart or if a few of the locals were in, a game was played. The games played were thirty-five or forty-five. The card drives at Christmas time were legendary. Word would get out that a turkey was being played for at the Kilmichael Bar. There was very little organisation needed as lots of people always turned up on the appointed evening. There was always enough space for them; tables were arranged and the games were played in the hushed silence of the bar. The spectators did not dare to interrupt the card players who took their game very seriously. Heaven help anybody who reneged or made a mistake; the cards were thrown down and sometimes the table was overturned in fury.

Each pub had its own regular card players – rather like the darts or snooker teams today – who played for their pub in 'away games'. The landlady was always part of these events. There was one memorable occasion when a group of card players from the KB travelled to Newcestown to play for a donkey. As they set off in three cars their main fear was that they might win the donkey and what could be done with it? The party included Mrs Shannon, Johnny Collins and Thomas Crean who declared it 'a brilliant night'. During the serious drinking which followed the card playing – thankfully, they didn't win the donkey, they came second – the owner of the pub was heard to say to one of his staff: 'Be careful now, don't let the Bandon crowd steal the glasses.' Johnny Collins, known for his witty comments, said in a disdainful tone: 'We drank out of more glasses than you ever saw.' This little incident did not deter the card players from playing at Newcestown again. Mrs Shannon and Denny Buttimer – the landlady's brother – were still meeting there at card games when Denny was ninety and Mrs Shannon was in her eighties.

Mary Shannon is now enjoying a well earned rest and a happy retirement with her son, Robert and his wife, Clare. She is a lady who is always cheerful and pleasant to everybody and is remembered fondly by the family who grew up in the Kilmichael Bar.

26

THE BOWLERS' TALE

Bandon can boast of many excellent bowlers: Denis Donovan, the supreme all round sportsman; Phil Searles, one of Bandon's best bowlers according to Barry Ellis; Donie Lehane and Joe Keohane, who lived in Foxes Street and excelled in the game; Corney Looney, a great junior bowler who did much for the game by organising tournaments 'up Foxes Street and down Monarone'; Finbarr Wilmot, one of the KB's most loved characters and another top-class bowler; Tommy Canniffe, a junior bowl player of some note; and Timmy Lawlor's father from Foxes Street, another one of 'Bandon's Bowling Hall of Fame'. John Joe Crean, from Raheroon near Bandon, defeated the famous Mick Barry in a tournament in Enniskeane and won a gold medal. His family donated a cup in his honour and the John Joe Crean Cup is now played for annually in Monarone.

Dinny Murphy, a quiet, unassuming man was one of Bandon's most respected players. He made his bowling debut as a senior bowler at Clancool in 1943 and reached the climax of his career in 1957 when he won the *Bol Cumann* All Ireland final against Seamus Fitzgerald at Tinker's Cross. 'There never was a more popular winner,' reported the sports journalist in the *Southern Star*. He was reputedly a superb bowler and a delight to watch, renowned for the accuracy and the speed of his shots. He was also a popular man and a very sporting chap. Flor Crowley, founder of *Bol Cumann* in 1954, who wrote in the *Southern Star* under the pseudonym 'Raymond', paid tribute to Dinny in the following words: 'It can be more truly said of him more than of any other man on the bowling road, that he has never lost a friend nor made an enemy in all his years as a bowler.' He went on to say that he would without hesitation, 'nominate Dinny Murphy as the greatest sportsman in the game of bowling.'

Bowling is played mainly with a twenty-eight ounce bowl made of iron. There is a choice of three weights: twenty-eight ounce, which is the norm, twenty-four ounce and sixteen-ounce. Bowling matches are called 'scores' because the winner is the person who covers the most ground in twenty shots. The referee tosses a coin to decide who has first throw. It is not an expensive sport, nor is it a team sport, but it certainly brought communities together on many a sunny Sunday after-noon in Phil's youth. The only requirements of the game are a bowl and a boreen – no fancy clothing or shoes. As a sport it is accessible to all. Traditionally, the game was played by local labourers, tenant farmers and tradesmen but never by the gentry. It is a game which has grown in adversity, there being many attempts to suppress it over the years and most recently in the 1920s. Lord Bandon broke rank and declared it 'a fine manly game'. He said that since 'scores were thrown in by-roads the bowlers were not causing any obstruction'. The game became more organised in 1932 with the founding of The All Ireland Bowling Association. Until the foundation of *Bol Cumann* in 1954 it was a parochial game with each parish supporting its own bowlers.

The bowling bishop, Cork's Bishop John Buckley, says that 'bowling is bred in our bones in Cork' but the origin of the game, which was originally known as 'Long Bullets', seems to be lost in the mists of time. There really is no evidence, according to Fintan Lane, in his excellent history of road bowling, *Long Bullets*, that road bowling existed in Ireland before the seventeenth century.

In 1884, Michael Cusack, one of the key founders of the GAA, listed bowling alongside hurling and football as a traditional Irish sport. Different areas of the country seem to have different techniques. In Cork, the full circle underarm swing known as the windmill technique – a run to the tip followed by a short jump as the bowl is thrown using a full circle arm motion – is favoured because it lofts the bowl keeping it high in the air during a large portion of the shot. The Armagh bowlers prefer a shorter approach run, a swift underarm shot causing the bowl to hit the road earlier at high speed. There are also different techniques for negotiating corners. In Cork, the bowler lofts the corner while in Armagh, the bowl spins and twists around the corner. The lofting technique is more suited to the bad road surfaces.

Road improvements and the increase in the volume of traffic have had a huge impact on the sport and many roads have fallen foul of urbanisation, consigning bowling to the margins. The tarring of roads for bowlers accustomed to rough surfaces was a difficult adjustment for them to make, therefore different skills were introduced. In the 1980s and 1990s Cork County Council was criticised for the size of the chips and fixatives being used on traditional bowling roads, hindering the sport which for many people in West Cork was their only social activity. The good bishop intervened on behalf of bowling, referring to it 'as a subculture with its own language and tradition'.

Gambling is very important to the game of bowling and high stakes are often set. At the beginning of a score the backers of each bowler divide into groups and open 'a book'. The names of the backers and their bets are recorded and when the total amount from each side is equal the score can begin. Sometimes the stakes are high but £2,000 to £4,000 is about the norm nowadays.

From her earliest years Phil can remember discussions in the KB about famous bowlers: Rocksalt Mahony, Tim Delaney, the Bennetts – Bill and George, Red Crowley and Mick Barry. The Barry family from Barryroe were outstanding bowl players according to Jerome Casey in his book, *Bowling Down London Way*. However, the cream of the bunch and 'the King of the Road' was Mick Barry, who is to bowling what Christy Ring is to hurling.

Mick lived in Waterfall and had the edge on the others because he was the one who lofted the ninety-nine foot high railway viaduct, just west of Cork, with a sixteen-ounce bowl, on St Patrick's Day in 1955. The two Bandonians, Denis Donovan and Donie Lehane, attempted it on the same day along with some other famous bowlers. Mick Barry retired from bowling in 1997. He was honoured by the Cork University where he had worked as a groundsman since he was fourteen years of age. He was given an honorary master of arts degree for his immense contribution to the world of sport – a well-deserved accolade to a man who had committed his whole life to the game, training and keeping himself physically fit. To his credit he was a life-long teetotaller.

Seánie Barry from Old Chapel was another well known local bowler. When he emigrated to America after the closure of the West Cork Railway in 1961 he took two bowls with him and introduced bowling to his corner of the New World. He is now well known in the Bronx for his bars and restaurants. It is heartening to know that so many of Bandon's emigrants did so well in their host countries. Seánie was the younger brother of Liam Barry who lived for a time in Shannon Street. Liam's wife, Nancy, was one of the first ladies to help with the cooking at the KB when the landlady opened the restaurant. In the late

1950s Liam and Nancy Barry emigrated to Co. Durham in the northeast of England.

By 1929, the Ford plant at Dagenham in Essex was fully operational and workers from Cork who relocated to the plant took the game with them to the highways and byways of Essex. The Ford Motor Company encouraged bowling among its workforce and provided generous sponsorship. Eugene McCarthy and Dan Murphy, both from Blarney Street, emigrated to London in 1939 owing to the lack of employment in Cork. They went to work at Ford's. Both being keen bowl players, they boarded the No. 87 bus one Sunday in 1940 and reconnoitred the roads of Essex looking for a suitable road on which to 'throw a score'. They discovered Launder's Lane in Rainham, a road which has become synonymous with bowling ever since. The following morning they made two cast iron bowls in the Ford foundry. That Sunday, having got permission from the local police force, the group on the Barking bus – Barking to Rainham – had swelled to twenty Corkonians. Continued immigration from Ireland, especially from Cork, swelled the ranks of the Launder's Lane bowlers. On Sundays after mass they boarded the No. 87 bus and headed off to Launder's Lane; bowling became a Sunday ritual for these emigrants just as it had been for them in their native Cork. The inaugural London Senior Championship was played in 1945 with thirty-two local competitors and by 1946, a junior tournament was introduced. The Bell Tavern in Barking became the venue for the presentation of prizes and the filling of cups.

27

THE TALE OF THE COBBLER'S WIFE

The name Nash has been associated with Bandon since the foundation of the town. It comes from the ash tree: strong and tall. One of the Nash ancestors, the bloodthirsty Captain Seán Dearg who was provost (mayor) of the town in the seventeenth century, bears no relation to the gentle people who lived in Shannon Street for many years.

The Nash family home was next door to the Kilmichael Bar. Mary and Thomas Nash had seven children. Their eldest son, Bobby, was well known for his wit and humour and had the opportunity to go to America in his younger days but preferred to remain in the family home. He was a very funny man and could keep the children of Foxes Street Cross amused for hours with his jokes and funny sayings, always ending with this party piece: 'I am like the fly at the heart of an apple, surrounded by sweetness, I'll dwell alone and die in singularity.' Michael was a baker employed by Brennan's. He later moved to Cork and worked for Thompsons' Confectioners. Timmy, who lived in Foxes Street, worked at the sand and gravel pit in the Distillery Road. Agnes, who married Timmy Whelton and moved across the road, had three children, Terry, Francis and Chrissie. Two girls, Lena and Chrissie, died as teenagers.

Lizzy Nash, a stunning young woman and the baby of the family, became the cook at the Cottage Hospital. She was renowned for her good, healthy food and for her kindness to the patients. She was the best neighbour a family could possibly have. If she lived today, she would certainly be presented with the 'Heart of Gold' award. She baked the Christmas cake for the landlady of the KB each Christmas while the children were young and she made a special Madeira cake for Marian who didn't like currants. Phil remembers the curds, whey and chicken broth this kind lady made for her and presented beautifully on a tray to tempt her taste buds when she was recovering from one of her bouts of illness.

Lizzy married Johnny Collins, a cobbler from Enniskeane who had served his time with Mr Seymour, a cobbler in North Main Street. He had lodgings with Molly Connell, who lived near Bandon Bridge. After the marriage, Johnny set up his shoemaker's shop in the Nash home. He was well known for the quality of his work and for his interest in greyhounds, which he trained for other people. He tells the story of how a farmer on his way to the mart rushed into his shop one day and dropped a bag on the counter, saying he would pick up the shoes therein next week when he returned to the mart. With the farmer still present Johnny opened the bag. It contained a litter of six pups! 'Oh Christ, I threw the wrong bag in the river,' wailed the farmer.

When her sister, Agnes, died, Lizzy left the Cottage Hospital to look after her family. She was anxious to give the seventeen-year-old Chrissie the opportunity to find work outside the home so that she could have some independence.

As soon as her services to this family were no longer required, she got a job as caretaker at the vocational school. She moved up as caretaker to the new school, St Brogan's, when it opened on the Macroom Road. It was a long journey from her home in Shannon Street but her nephew, Finbarr, was kind and regularly took her to work or picked her up. She worked there until her final illness.

Lizzy fought a brave battle against cancer but sadly the disease defeated her in the end. Phil felt she could identify with the sentiments expressed by the young man depicted in the song 'The Old Bog Road' because she could not attend Lizzy's funeral. She had an important part to play in the town pantomime in Milford Haven at that precise time – a frivolous reason to miss the funeral of such a loyal friend. As a result, Phil never again took part in a stage production. After she left the convent, Lizzy was there for her twenty-four hours a day to listen, to advise and to accompany her to town on really bad days. Her kindness has never been forgotten.

She was well known and loved by generations of children who grew up in the vicinity of Foxes Street Cross. No doubt many of them can recount stories of her kindness. She lived her life as a generous and loyal friend to all who had the privilege of knowing her.

28

THE CHILDREN'S TALE

To the children brought up in Shannon Street, Boyle Street and Foxes Street in the 1940s and 1950s, Foxes Street Cross was their playground. It was safe to play in the middle of the road because there were so few cars and the road was so wide. Phil recalls the days when, as lively youngsters, they had skipping ropes reaching from one side of Shannon Street to the other and they could skip for hours without being disturbed. It was the same with football, except that this carried the fear of breaking a window. Another popular ball game was played against the gable end of the Kilmichael Bar; it involved hitting the ball with the flat of the hand against the wall. There were certain other intricacies involved in this game but they are now forgotten.

All the children knew each other by name and played together happily, always on the lookout for each other. The winter snow was eagerly looked forward to. The tap at the top of Foxes Street would be turned on so that the water from it would freeze and the children could skate down the street on trays. They had no thought for the elderly whose lives were in danger when they went to draw water. There was no running water in most of the houses back then. Only the low wall outside Johnny Barrett's home kept people from ending up in his hallway. Johnny, father of Jim and Corney, who were often part of the game, was a cobbler and an ex-British army officer. Some of the men would throw hot ashes on the ice to melt it to make the road safe for people.

As the children grew older they ventured further afield down to the Twigs, a willow grove near the railway line where the films seen in Jackie Brien's cinema the previous week would be re-enacted. Bows and arrows or swords were cut from twigs. There was much climbing and swinging from trees all accompanied by lots of shouting and laughter. In summer the children moved in gangs to John O'Mahony's stream, equipped with jam jars, string and little fishing nets attached to bamboo sticks, where they whiled away a fine afternoon paddling in the stream and catching cols: a type of minnow used in fishing. Whatever was caught was put back in the water before they departed. Swimming in the bogs was another of the summer pursuits. The majority of Bandonians who learned to swim in those days learned in the Bandon River before it reached the town, in an area called 'the Bogs' at the back of Castle Road.

Minister Brown's steps at the top of Foxes Street were a place where more sedentary activities took place. Stories were narrated or daisy chains were made from daisies collected earlier. Occasionally, tired of sitting, a game of 'kiss and chase' was played on the minister's avenue. If the publican ever noticed that his flock was missing and decided he did not want them playing on the street when they should be attending to their homework he would appear at the corner and shout their names in descending order and in they would have to go. However, as soon as the da got busy in the bar or was chatting to somebody, his offspring escaped through the wicket gate and back to join their friends on the steps.

The railway was a great place in which to play. Here there were obstacles to be overcome and tanks to be climbed until the station master gave chase and then it was a scuttle up the path and over the gate to the safety of home. On one occasion Phil's brother, Pat, accompanied by Teddy Lucitt, was playing down the railway. Both climbed up on some water tanks and of course the inevitable happened – they fell in. Mother Mahony was beside herself when she saw the state of her eldest son, realising that the children could have drowned easily; no doubt Mrs Lucitt suffered the same anguish. The railway was out of bounds for the KB kids for many weeks until the incident was forgotten.

Tins, pots, pans, bin lids and chamber pots were retrieved from a rubbish heap beside the railway gates and groups of boys walked up and down the street banging them with sticks or stones. It was a great evening's entertainment – they called themselves the Rusty Bucket Band. They made more noise than music but they were safe and creatively engaged.

Walking was also a great pastime: down the Innishannon Road, up to the Four Crosses, around Baldwin's Bridge and returning via Monarone – a good six or seven mile hike.

Castle Bernard was a jaunt for Sunday afternoons as it involved a long journey through the town and out the New Road almost as far as Old Chapel, before the children could enjoy a game of hide and seek in the castle grounds or pick rhododendrons from the avenue.

The arrival of the circus was a huge event. Some of the boys helped put up the Big Top to obtain free tickets. Before the matinee even started the field was visited to view the animals. Before the days of television the circus provided the only opportunity the children had to see exotic animals; there were lions, tigers and elephants, as well as the beautiful white stallions and the performing dogs. The circus folk drank in the KB between shows and this was very exciting for the children of the family, especially Barry, Phil's youngest brother, who as a little boy was amazed to see the dwarfs, who were smaller than he was, drinking pints! These men worked very hard putting up and taking down the Big Top. They got up at four o'clock in the morning and were on their way before the townspeople woke up.

Joe Keohane's step was the venue for 'pitch and toss', which was played mainly by the men and boys. Joe's uncle, Pat Chambers, veteran of the Spanish Civil War, enjoyed this game. On a memorable Sunday morning while a group were engrossed in their game, somebody threw eggs from a house across the road. The eggs landed on Johnny Brien's head and ran down his new 'Sunday going to mass suit'. The air in Foxes Street was blue that morning. Pontoon, also favoured by Pat Chambers, was played on the same steps, Johnny Collins having taught generations of youngsters how to play.

Carnival Week opened with the children's fancy dress parade which started at the Shambles and ended at the Bogs. In the days before the opening of the Charlie Hurley Park all sporting events, as well as other gatherings, were held there. During carnival week, which was a real community effort, there was a hurling or football match. Pipers and later Perks Amusements set up shop at the Shambles, with their music blasting out through the town. Every night children and adults flocked there for a turn on the swing boats, the dodgems and the other rides on offer. The adults had a go at the various side shows trying to win a goldfish or coconut for their over-excited children. Added to this were the nightly gatherings at the boys' club with more games and raffles.

The big fancy dress parade on the Wednesday night brought thousands of people to town. This was a great event which started at Foxes Street Cross and gave the KB float an advantage. It could be prepared in the yard then just appear as the parade was starting. The parade was held in September and started around nine o'clock when it was dusk. The route was lit by lights which people set up in their bedroom windows to shine directly on the parade. It was magical. A young woman from the town was chosen as carnival queen and was attended by four or five ladies in waiting. It was a great honour to be chosen for these roles but it involved a busy week for the queen and her retinue, presiding at events, presenting prizes, drawing raffles and leading the parades on Sunday and Wednesday. Phil remembers Jean Sullivan from Foxes Street and Maureen O'Leary from Distillery Road as carnival queens. Mickey Cohalan's sister, Colette (Good), was carnival queen in 1946 for the second carnival. The first carnival was held in 1945 and it was still going strong in the early 1960s. It was the best week of the year in Bandon and was looked forward to eagerly. All the main businesses in the town entered floats of a very high standard; Beamish's float was a blaze of colour and music and the church choir also had a very colourful float with, of course, some superb singing.

As well as the annual Corpus Christi procession, there was the May procession in the beautiful convent grounds. The girls looked forward to this, expectantly wondering who would be chosen to crown Our Lady or throw flower petals along the route of the procession. Girls brought armfuls of flowers to school. The 'bouquets' were dismantled and the petals put in beautiful long handled baskets to be strewn by a chosen dozen of the first communicants, resplendent in their white dresses and veils. A leaving certificate girl carried the crown around the grounds and then placed it on the statue of Mary while everybody sang Marian hymns, the main favourite being:

Bring flowers of the rarest, Bring blossoms the fairest
From garden and woodland and hillside and dale
Our full hearts are swelling, our glad voices telling
The praise of the loveliest flower of the May.
O Mary we crown thee with blossoms today
Queen of the Angels and Queen of the May.

Another big event at the convent was when the nuns visited from Texas. Presentation Convent Bandon had founded a convent in San Antonio, Texas, in the early 1950s and thereafter a few of the sisters working in the USA would return to Bandon annually for a holiday. Mother Peter Corcoran was a relative of the Kilmichael Bar family and Phil always looked forward to her visits. There was a concert in the convent garden where all the nuns sat around and the schoolgirls entertained them with songs, poems, dancing and musical items. In return, the children were allowed to play in the convent garden. The yanks, as visitors from America were called in those days, would present the 'entertainers' with luscious sweets in recognition of their efforts.

Throughout those long summer's evenings the children lived life to the full with the freedom and security which is their birthright. It seems light years away from the television and computer games which impoverish the lives of our young people today – lives strongly influenced by soap opera stars. Money was scarce in Phil's youth but the children never noticed. The wealth of experience, creative opportunity, humour and talent they had more than compensated for any material shortage. The Foxes Street Cross children of the 1940s, 1950s and 1960s grew to be hard working, well adjusted citizens who helped to make Bandon the community-spirited and friendly town it still is today.

Phil grew to love her adopted home in Milford Haven where she married and raised a son but the ties which bind her to Bandon can never be severed, just as the wonderful characters whom she knew and loved there can never be forgotten. Her rich childhood in the Kilmichael Bar was populated by characters, the likes of whom she shall never meet again. Phil lived at a period when people mattered to each other and shared what little they had. She has told the stories to her son, Neil, over the years. He has known and loved Pat and Nora Wilmot all his life, just as Phil has. He bumped into Saxy Dan in a Glasgow pub recently where they had a pint together. Hopefully he will tell the stories to his children, thereby ensuring that these great people of Bandon and the Kilmichael Bar will continue to live on through their stories and keep the wicket gate open for future generations.

ACKNOWLEDGEMENTS

The writing of a book is the work of many people and certainly this work could not have been completed without the assistance of my many friends and family who supported the project from the beginning. To all of them I offer my gratitude and love. Thanks to those whose stories are included here for the generous and honest way in which you shared your life experiences with me, I consider it a sacred trust to do you justice. To those who told me stories of their loved ones I also consider a sacred trust to do justice to their memories.

To the many of you who talked to me, live or on tape, to those who helped in so many ways you know who you are and you also know that I really am appreciative of your assistance.

A few who went beyond the loyalty of family and friendship:

My Mercy sisters: Sister Finbarr and Sister Gabriel who made sense of my convoluted sentences and their able assistants Sister Patricia and Sister Immaculata, their love and encouragement is a constant in my life.

My readers and advisors on the manuscript: Tim Barrett, Pat Clark, Teifryn Williams, Frank O'Mahony and Neil Walters.

Eddie Goggin of the *Bandon Opinion* has been with this project from the beginning and been generous with his support and permission to use articles from that excellent publication, which keeps those of us who are exiles informed about what is happening at home The *Bandon Opinion* has gone from strength to strength over the years thanks to Eddie's enthusiasm and hard work.

My thanks to that great Bandonian – Paddy Connolly – sadly no longer with us; his contribution to the town is without equal. May he rest in peace. Thanks to his son Pat for his permission to use extracts from Paddy's excellent book *Bandon – 400 Years of History.*

Barry Ellis' telephone will have a rest now that the book is complete! He has been brilliant – interviewing people, thinking of information I might find helpful and making lists. His assistance with the information regarding our war heroes has been truly informative, I am ashamed of my own lack of knowledge regarding the lives of Phil Searles, the Walsh brothers and the Barrett family; regulars of the KB who had suffered so much. To Billy Good thanks to you and Barry and members of the War Memorial Committee for permission to use extracts from your informative book *A Journey of Remembrance* and *Bandon and District and the First World War.*

Thanks to Padraig Hamilton for his assistance with his father's story as well as allowing me to use information from the Bandon Historical Society. Also to John Merwick for permission to quote from his informative book, *History of Bandon Rugby Club*.

Thanks to Noreen, Denis and Norienne Lehane for all their assistance. Thanks also to Celia O'Brien and Anthony Cohalan.

Ken Watson thanks for sharing his nautical expertise and to Michael Galvin for sharing his research into the Swete Estate, thank you both.

Without my computer guru, John booth, this book would never have been completed.

My friend Donal Murphy of *The Cork Examiner*; thank you. To Leo McMahon of the *Southern Star*; thank you. They both 'dug out' articles from their respective papers.

Con Houlihan; thank you for doing me the honour of writing the excellent foreword.

Mary Feehan and her team at Mercier press for their patience and tolerance – it has been a pleasure working with them.

Lastly thanks to David and Neil for their ever present love and support.

BIBLIOGRAPHY

Begley, Diarmuid, *The Road to Crossbarry* (Deso Publications, Bandon, 1999)

Bennett, George, *History of Bandon* (Henry and Coghlan, Cork, 1862)

Brehony, Tony, *West Cork* (A B Books, Dublin, 2001)

Casey, Jerome, *Bowling Down London Way* (self published, 1996)

Connolly, Paddy, *Bandon: 400 years of history* (self published, 2000)

Coogan, Tim Pat, *Where Ever Green Is Worn – The Story of the Irish Diaspora* (Hutchinson, London, 2000)

Dunne, Catherine, *An Unconsidered People: The Irish in Sixties London* (New Island Books, Dublin, 2003)

Good, William and Ellis, *Barry* (eds), A Journey of Remembrance – Walks in the Footsteps of Bandon Soldiers (Bandon War Memorial Committee, Bandon, 2005)

Lane, Fintan, *Long Bullets: A History of Road Bowling in Ireland* (Galley Head Press, West Cork, 2005)

Laxton, Edward, *The Famine Ships: Irish Exodus to America, 1846-51* (Bloomsbury Publishing PLC, London, 1997)

Merwick, John, *History of Bandon Rugby Club* (self published, 1982)

O' Donoghue, Florence, *Rebel Corks Fighting Story* (Anvil Press, Kerry, 1961)

O'Broin, Leon, *No Man's Man* (Institute of Public Administration, Dublin, 1982)

O'Donoghue, Denis, *History of Bandon* (Cork Historical Guides Committee, Cork, 1970)

O'Mahony Walters, Johanna, *Merci Beaucoup*, (self published, 2001)

Newspapers and Journals
Bandon Historical Journal Number 11
Bandon Historical Journal Number 3
Bandon Opinion Christmas editions 1980s –
Bandon Opinions 1970s 1980s 1990s
Cork Examiner February 1979
Southern Star circa 1916/1917